THE SOLITARY OUTLAW

THE SOLITARY OUTLAW

BY B.W. POWE

LESTER
&ORPEN
DENNYS
PUBLISHERS

First Edition
Second Printing: 1987

All inquiries regarding motion picture, television, or related rights in
or to this book should be addressed to the Author's representative,
The Colbert Agency Inc., 303 Davenport Road, Toronto, Canada, M5R 1K5.
Representations as to the disposition of these rights without the express
written consent of the Author's representative are strictly prohibited.

Canadian Cataloguing in Publication Data

Powe, B.W. (Bruce W.), 1955-
The solitary outlaw

ISBN 0-88619-141-6.

1. Intellectuals - Canada.   2. Intellectuals.
I. Title.

HM213.P69 1987   305.5'52'0971   C87-093427-9

Jacket and interior design by
Thadaney Wittermann Design Communications

Typeset at Lester & Orpen Dennys using PageOne™ desktop
publishing software with the McCutcheon Graphics Pages™
Macintosh™ SE computer system.

Printed and bound in Canada

Lester & Orpen Dennys Limited
78 Sullivan Street
Toronto, Ontario
M5T 1C1

For Deborah

CONTENTS

Burning Books.....................9

The Solitary Outlaw...............19

The Quiet Civil War of Pierre Trudeau.....69

A Search for Glenn Gould...............135

Apprehensions Now: Canetti and McLuhan.....167

Acknowledgements...............191

BURNING
BOOKS

1

Burning books. A burning library.

Pyres celebrate the death of the humanist enlightenment and the triumph of Mass Man. The books provide the Speer-headed sparks.

Then a scholar in a frenzy turns on his life work. He pulls down shelves, builds a mound of books, and shouts, "Fire".

Two images: two events. One is from Elias Canetti's *Die Blendung*, or *The Blinding*; the other is history itself, imagined by that novel.

Now on the street. Night: the electric rhythms from ghetto blasters and late-night bars. Dance steps. Trance steps. Blue lights flicker on the windows and curtains of shut-in homes. Cars speed by, tapedecks snapping out snatches of the same sound you hear on your own radio. The street is never serene. Laser beams on towers sweep the sky. Crowds watch each other as if waiting for someone to perform. It is a Disneyland of pleasurable attractions and distractions. Who can keep away?

On a corner, a bookstore is lit up and busy. On the windows posters announce

BINS OF BOOKS

LIQUIDATION

40% TO 50% OFF

BIG SALE

BOOKS—CHEAP!!!

Major items offered: dictionaries. *The Oxford English Dictionary* (abridged), Funk and Wagnall, Random House, Webster, and a reprint of Samuel Johnson.

A dictionary is a depository of fragments, a collection and collation of bits. Out of these fragments, can words form into something to be preserved or into something easily forgettable?

2

Wyndham Lewis, Marshall McLuhan, Pierre Elliott Trudeau, Glenn Gould, and Elias Canetti.

Lewis: an internationalist who was a Canadian, of sorts.

McLuhan, Trudeau, Gould: three Canadians who were internationalists.

Canetti: a winner of the Nobel Prize for Literature in 1981, a displaced central European now living in England, an author who tried to speak out to all.

These are men who have felt the power, passion, and accountability of words.

Canetti says in *The Play of the Eyes* (1986)

> I could not forgive myself for burning the books....I felt that I had sacrificed not only my own books but also those of the whole world, for the sinologist's library included everything of importance to the world....All that had burned, I had let it happen, I had made no attempt to save any part of it.

A civilized conscience shows in the tactics the five took to counter the burning books, the threatened obsolescence of print: McLuhan, through teaching; Lewis, through provocation of his readers; Trudeau, through political action and debate; Gould, in meditation and solitude; Canetti, in the study of the crowd and the dissolution of the individual "I" into the mass.

All are private men who went outside into their society. This tension between privacy and publicity is a source of their strength, and of their complexity. For they are divided men who often contained within themselves the turbulence of their time and place. Once they had gone outside into their society, away from a private centre, they assumed what Canetti calls an acoustic mask: a play of "I's", a drama of words, a forum of questions and perceptions.

Each tried to understand the role of rational and humane action in an irrational, self-destructive world; each saw communication between individuals as a necessity; and when each returned to privacy or silence, he remained resistant to an easy scan of his character.

All five were engaged in contact with the post-literate society.

3

Literacy: the ability to read and interpret the written word.

What is post-literacy? It is the condition of semi-literacy, where most people can read and write to some extent, but where the literate sensibility no longer occupies a central position in culture, society, and politics. Post-literacy occurs when the ability to comprehend the word decays.

If post-literacy is now the ground of society, then questions arise:

What happens to the reader, the writer, and the book in the post-literate environment?

What happens to thinking, resistance, and dissent when the ground becomes wordless, electric, and musical?

If the literate sensibility is being erased, then it could be that the private self—one of the supreme accomplishments of western society—will vanish with it. We have yet to understand to what extent the self-conscious "I" was created by the print medium, what McLuhan called "The Gutenberg Galaxy".

4

Yet we are the children of electricity, and post-literacy is our frontier. There are writers who have refused to be impotent when faced with the decline of the word, the burning of books. There are intellectuals who have tried to transcend the depersonalizing drift of society by using literacy as a force of critical consciousness. These are people who have chosen to affect a time that may be rejecting the play of words in print.

5

Lewis, Trudeau, Gould, Canetti, McLuhan: this eclectic combination of intellectuals—all obsessed by techniques of communication, all absorbed in finding readers and receivers, all intent on provoking debate—can teach us about challenging the world with a torrent of words or a well-aimed blast. Each set out to discover ways of understanding, charts for rereading the technological ground of our time; each moved out into the post-literate frontier of society. The dissimilarities between the five figures are greater than the similarities. You will not find categorical connections here. But they share this: all wanted to deal urgently with the implications of mass society for books, music, politics, culture, and individual thinking itself. For each the most annoying word in the English language is "relax".

THE SOLITARY
OUTLAW

1

MERELY A PERSON

I am here.
Czeslaw Milosz

Picture a fate: in a room Percy Wyndham Lewis writes alone. Location: Flat A, 29 Kensington Garden Studios, Notting Hill Gate, London. The building's status: condemned. Decade: the 1950s. Mood: as if we are inhabiting the remains of the Nagasaki blast. "There is no movement gathered here," Lewis wrote in *The Enemy,* No. 1, "merely a person; a solitary outlaw and not a gang." The blind man writes downward until his pen slips off the pad. Then the page is ripped out and dropped to the floor. There it collects with other papers: notes for a new novel. His library smells like dust and mildew, old books and ink.

Why demand controversy?

"I have moved outside," Lewis had announced in 1927, "in solitary schism....I can resume my opinion of the society I have just left." He is the self-appointed critic of all that seeks to suppress reason. Stubbornly, Lewis ignores the eviction threats. The building's sole occupant, with his wife, he often feels like the last of his—critical—kind. His uncompleted drawings and paintings are locked in backrooms. Only by writing can this mere person stay awake. "All other times have bred criticism, and its wholesome revolts...only this time exacts an uncritical hypnotic sleep."

Location change: Toronto, 1943. Season: winter. A confinement cell for the intellect: the Tudor Hotel. There were two Toronto addresses: Apt. 11A, 559 Sherbourne Street, now a shopping mall offering video rentals, dry cleaning, and submarine sandwiches; and a studio at 22 Grenville Street until 1941, now the Ontario Coroner's Office, euphemism for city morgue. In this Siberia of the Soul, the hotel burns down, obliterating Lewis's papers and books. "It was a fiery spectre," he wrote, "a fiery iceberg."

Dissolve to: the London flat slated for demolition. The "defender of western man" who had flirted with authoritarian forces, admired Hitler and then recanted, warned about dangers in the twentieth century, from Peter Pans to puppet robots, from the persuasive press to pervasive radio and film—new modes of repercussion, new makes of being (from the Anglophone to the telephone)—from the Bloomsbury cliques to the pull and push of money power (for Lewis, all things politically impend), a man who wrote ill-advised throwaways with titles like *The Jews: Are They Human?*, and who came to doubt the existence of others—and of himself—this writer finishes a novel in which he turns an Honest Eye on himself. In mid-century (1954) the novel is produced. The title: *Self-Condemned.*

A self-acknowledged renegade, Lewis defies from a distance. "I am issuing a challenge to the community in which I live," he said in *Time and Western Man* (1927).

"I am criticizing its institutions and modes of advice and thought. I create 'disgust'."

SYMPATHY FOR THE DEVIL

"You should be reading [pause] Wyn-damn Lewis. Not a great writer. But a great satirist.... Very witty. His writings you see are designed like a vortex. Of course most people haven't noticed this. So...start with *The Art of Being Ruled...* and uh... [lapse] *Men Without Art....* Yes. I knew him. When he was at Windsor."

So Marshall McLuhan introduced the outcast from the group dubbed by Lewis "the men of 1914", the unknown among academic reputation machines called Pound, Eliot, and Joyce. If these authors formed the official litera- ture, then somehow Lewis didn't fit in. His name was treated like news that cancer can be communicated with a handshake.

I followed McLuhan's suggestion and over the years began to scour bookstores to find copies of Lewis's novels and essays. Booksellers stared at me in stunned surprise.

Did I mean D.B. Wyndham Lewis, the historian and co-author with Charles Bennett of Hitchcock's *The Man Who Knew Too Much*? Or did I mean C.S. Lewis? Then again, maybe I meant John Wyndham, author of *Day of the Triffids*.

Clarification.

"Oh...the fascist."

Lewis's reputation existed in secondhand bookstores among collectors who debated backlists as if they were whispering holy writ.

Other writers didn't help. "That snarling authoritar- ian," Irving Howe said; "a crank...a completely negative thinker," a scholar judged in a work I had on Pound and Eliot.

But my search continued. Next: the Lewis entries at Toronto's Central and Robarts libraries—Fort Book, as the latter is known. The entries cited more than forty volumes, including poems, plays, travelogues, and memoirs.

Then I found his philosophy books: brittle editions with titles like *The Diabolical Principle and the Dithyrambic Spectator* and *Paleface*. My first readings were strained. For someone like myself with liberal humanist aspirations, Lewis's ideas seemed cruel. His anti-narrative technique had a strange effect; his writing rarely seemed to flow forward. But his style had power. His words put you on alert. It was as if he were grabbing you by the throat, asking you to reply, even...to stop.

Information came slowly.

Birth Date: November 18, 1882.

Birth Place: Amherst, Nova Scotia, in a yacht.

Nationality: regarded as British, sometimes American. Carried a Canadian passport. Opinion of birthplace: "an unspeakable national zero."

Marriage Status: one wife, Anne, called Froanna.

Children: several, apparently; all illegitimate.

Paintings and Drawings: collections at the Tate Gallery in England; the War Museum (Ottawa); in private collections and small galleries in England, the United States, Canada. A coffee-table book was published in 1971.

Camouflage and Projections: The Enemy, The Tyro; nicknamed "Wind ham" and "Wind 'em"; "the only prose writer among my contemporaries to create a new, an original prose style" (T.S. Eliot), with "the eyes...of an unfulfilled rapist" (Hemingway), "the man who was wrong about everything except the superiority of live mind to dead mind" (Pound); founder of Vorticism, *Blast,* and the Rebel Art Centre, 18 Great Ormond Street, Queen's Square, hours—11:00 a.m. to 1:00 p.m. "I am an artist,"

Lewis introduced himself in *Blasting and Bombardiering* (1937), "if that is credential. I am a novelist, painter, sculptor, philosopher, draughtsman, critic, politician, journalist, essayist, pamphleteer, all rolled into one...."

Death: March 7, 1957, London.

Publishing Status: that of a manuscript culture.

Friends pass hardback and paperback finds to other friends, first editions are photocopied and stored in plastic covers on shelves, Lewis is debated in dark bars and dens, and the image of the artist is formed from Hugh Kenner's *The Pound Era* and other source books.

1984: in Toronto's *Globe and Mail*

WRONG-ABOUT-EVERYTHING MAN MAY BE MAKING A COMEBACK

Two years after the centenary of his birth, I saw a modest revival underway in England and the United States. Revaluations of Lewis's work were available in Toronto: one interesting—*Fables of Aggression: The Modernist as Fascist* (1979) by Fredric Jameson; the other timid—*The Enemy* (1980), a biography by Jeffrey Meyers. In California, Black Sparrow Press republished *Blast 1* and *2* (and added *3*), *Self-Condemned*, *The Apes of God*, and later the apologia, *Rude Assignment: A Narrative of My Career Up-to-Date*. Lewis himself had a guest shot in Anthony Burgess's *Earthly Powers*, where he appeared like a spectre lurking in the shadows of cultural history.

The opponent of the anonymous was back.

Almost.

THE SOLITARY OUTLAW

Why books?...Nutrition of impulse.
Ezra Pound

This slow introduction shows how long it took me to recover Wyndham Lewis, and to understand what he had said. Ironically, Lewis expected retaliation. "All you need to be is a practised shot!" This Great Opposition Force needed a responsive public. "I am only concerned with *effects,*" he said in *Time and Western Man.* The effect he came to foreshadow: the situation of the writer in the post-literate milieu.

What does it mean to say the context of the word is post-literate? We see vast shifts: when there is a decline in the sense of a reader, a public becomes a market to be guided and sold; patronage for publishing is necessary through government, university, and corporate sponsorship; intellectual salons become faculty clubs; a text becomes furniture ("the coffee-table book") or a floppy disk; post-literacy is the condition of publishers, editors, and even writers themselves; and serious writing seems to become an underground manuscript culture. Distribution, high printing costs, the lack of comprehensive education: these control what a writer can say or do. In North America, an author who pursues the market can publish almost anything and his message will be trivialized by the sensationalist media, the TV twist. This is the signal of the massage: "You may say what you want, but nothing means anything."

Any question of the role of the word, of books, of mind, cannot be new. We give words their currency by entry into our own time's arena. So in Canada, a laboratory of the western world where the advance effects of technological conditions can be felt, we note how the publishing industry suffers from the absence of a real public. Publishers slash lists; and the grant system dominates. Since most authors feel isolated, there is a risk that crying "foul" will sound precious. But our fear is justified when the circulation of the word is threatened by blockage and bankruptcy. GO AHEAD…CANCEL, a word-processor tells its user. And at the touch of a key: oblivion.

In a flash of analogy, we see how Lewis's work was cancelled by the depersonalizing forces he confronted. The irony: what he demanded from his readers was a strong point-of-view, concentrated debate, and resistance to the killers of the human spirit. "All forms of art of a permanent order," he said in *Men Without Art* (1934), "are intended not only to please and excite, believe me, Plain Reader, if you are still there, but to call into play the entire human capacity for sensation, reflection, imagination, and will."

It is hard to assess an author whose writings are mostly unavailable. There is no public memory of P. Wyndham Lewis. With certain writers you have to read a lot of their work before you can approach what they say. So it was only after thinking over *Tarr, Time and Western Man, The Art of Being Ruled,* and *Self-Condemned,* that his message came through.

His defence of intelligence begins and ends in words, and for words.

> Hatred of *the word* goes hand in hand with hatred of the intellect, for *the word* is, of course, its sign. Language is one of the things to be broken up—a stammer, a hiatus, an ellipsis, a syncope, a hiccup, is installed in the midst of a verb, and the mind attacked through its instrument. *(The Art of Being Ruled)*

For Wyndham Lewis, the Solitary Outlaw is the literate person in the post-literate society. Or: if you are conscious and intelligent, you are outside the mainstream.

The Solitary Outlaw is you—the reader of your time, the critic of your surroundings.

INDEPENDENT MIND

Remember Lewis as one of "the men of 1914" for whom writing meant a blast of new criticism and a revival of creative force and form. He was the first of his group to be forgotten, and he is the last to be forgiven. If I recall him here, it is because he can help us define what is lost when society obliterates the effects of the print medium.

Lewis identified literacy with individuality: with consciousness, choice, and the ability to reason. Critics will tell us that there is no hard empirical evidence for that belief. Yet his more than fifty books reveal how he was obsessed with the way words shape the critical "I".

The printed word was his link to the independent mind. Without print, there could be no possibility of thought and dialogue. Without words, you could not think around the signals of your age. "The intellect," Lewis says in *The Art of Being Ruled,* "is more removed from the crowd than is anything; but it is not a snobbish withdrawal, but a going aside for the purpose of work." Strip us of literate speech and we become mute and cannot speak out. The post-literate society would reduce us to a tribal mass that offers no chance for individual dissent. The post-literate milieu would use wordlessness to control the free intellect. "The life of intelligence is the very incarnation of freedom," Lewis says. He insists that there is a psychic need for the charge of the word to expose the false fronts of the world and permit the reader and writer to view their existence with clarity and brilliance.

Whether Lewis's ideas could be confirmed by neural science, psychology, or cultural history may not matter.

The metaphor of votive speech is his imperative. He began his artistic life with the belief that literature could create a *siècle de lumière*, a century of light, by the power of its purpose.

How far away that responsibility seems.

We are the first men of a future that has not material-ized. We belong to a great age that has not come off. We moved too quickly for the world. We set too sharp a pace. And, more and more, exhausted by war, slump, and revolution, the world has fallen back. Its ambition has withered. *(Blasting and Bombardiering)*

That was Lewis's challenge and his warning. His realism (generally misread as pessimism) was the result of his being at the front lines of political movements and ideas, and of having watched artists die or be starved into submissive silence.

Today when we are faced with post-literacy and a computerized-corporate culture that seems to have less and less use for any individualized art, we must question where our written missiles will go. The conscience of the time often seems crippled by the paralysing presence of another "empire of the sun", the title of J.G. Ballard's masterwork and an image of the impact of the Nagasaki bomb; ours is a false *siècle de lumière* that comes from the light of a nuclear meltdown or raid.

But annihilation is the key to Lewis, too.

He always went against every current he feared. His writings are incoherent and flailing, like the sputtering of someone drowning in a destructive tide. The more he shouted and waved his arms, the more energy and friction he generated. Yet he said to those who would come after him: "I believe that at some future date I shall have my niche in the Bolshevist pantheon…to show how repulsive unbridled individualism can be."

2

FIND THE ENEMY

Picture: a World War I battlefield. Shells shrieking. Flat
tack of a machine gun. Flares burst and offer a brief vision
of the field. Wrecks, ruins, flames. Tangled wire. The stink
of powder and gunpits. Two observers in a trench gaze out
on the landscape. Their equipment: binoculars, maps, and
flashlights. The two share alarm at the decay and stench
around them. Shells slam into the earth. Shadowy troops
move. Each observer hopes one of them will carry on
with the reconnaissance. The rude assignment: find out the
news. The reason: no one is sure.

Lewis said in the 1920s, after the war he had fought in

For a very complete and profound inundation is at
hand. After *us* comes the Deluge: more probably than
not, however, before that, and out of its epigram-
matic sequence. Meantime, we have a duty where the
officials of the Flood, as they might be called, are concerned. We have to serve them out with gas-masks,
light navigable craft of a seaworthy and inconspicuous

type, and furnish them with instructions as to currents, winds, head-swells, maritime effluvia, sargasso seas, doldrums, sharks, waterspouts, and sea-serpents. The complete equipment of an inspector of the Flood would be of such a technical description that it is impossible, however, to more than hint at it. *(The Art of Being Ruled)*

He became The Enemy in order to know the enemy. His essays, novels, polemics, poems, and plays form a single inquiry into the murderous currents of the mass-age. But for him to find the enemies of life, he had to devise a way of seeing them. He made a method. Which is: characterize the atmosphere of your time. Consciously exaggerate objects of attention so that they become grotesque and therefore laughable. (Laughter insures a measure of distance.) Confront how we exist in cultural-political arenas and our lack of awareness of that environment's impact. Only a slave dances to the jerk of invisible strings. Only a slave lines up to be slaughtered without asking why.

Lewis used his trained eye of a painter to visualize the control of modern life by machines and the crowd mentality. He was devoted to a radical critique of the effect of cultural, political, and intellectual systems on the individual. "If, however, one artist, and a single child are preserved intact and unpolluted owing to my words, I should consider my pains richly rewarded."

The Lewisite method is confusingly articulated in *The Art of Being Ruled* (1926). Here he takes Machiavelli's *The Prince* and Machiavellian techniques of leadership (the latter the subject of his 1927 study of Shakespeare and heroes, *The Lion and the Fox*) and applies these principles to readership. If Machiavelli advised politicians on the art of ruling, then Lewis advised citizens on the techniques of critical intelligence. The book is a training manual in attitude: "not intended for the docile consumer."

The Art of Being Ruled is in fact a fragment from one large work titled *The Man of the World*. This oversized missile was to include philosophy, fiction, memoir, criticism, and essay—an opus huge enough to block the twentieth-century rush towards suicide. Lewis's publishers, with sensitive foresight, rejected the scale of the project, and so he hammered the whole into pieces. Commentators repeat those editors' mistakes: they chisel his output into manageable bits. *Time and Western Man, Paleface, The Art of Being Ruled,* and *The Childermass* (1928) are the remains of his "key" to open "this plausible 'life' that is often not life."

In *The Enemy of the Stars* (1915), Lewis had announced his intentions to the reader in his "Programme Notes"

VERY WELL ACTED BY YOU AND ME

This was his contract with the *"hypocrite lecteur"*, his invitation to YOU AND ME to search for a true liberty.

Look behind his blastings and blessings, and you will find that his touchstone is eighteenth-century high literacy, "that phantom of democratic enlightenment". His Plain Reader is a variation on Johnson's Common Reader. Lewis's satire (hyperbole and ridicule) is a therapeutic enema for social poison. "Constant measures have to be taken against bad air…this is hygiene."

In *Rude Assignment* (1950), Lewis admits that his intentions were misunderstood. But his "intellectual memoir" restates his "Advice to the Inmates of the Power-house": "Socially life in the modern age is like being in an immense building full of a radioactive something we call 'power'. It is 'malignant'…and we are all slightly 'cancered'."

What was his advice?

Find out what is being done, and to whom. Stand close to history; but not so close that you will be swallowed. "The well-adjusted man is a robot," he said. If you go with the flow, then you could become mindless. If you stay anonymous when you are aware of what is going on, then you give automatic assent to whomever is in authority. To be a passive member of any club, crowd, or party is to be dead. New social crises require a new weaponry of words. In short, the Plain Reader should not be plain at all.

> In our society two virtues are badly contrasted, that of the *fighter* and *killer*...and that of the *civilizer* and *maker*...It is hoped that certain things that have flown a grey neutral flag will be forced to declare themselves as...the dark or the light. *(The Art of Being Ruled)*

For the art of being ruled is the art of not being fooled. By anyone or anything.

EFFICIENT CHIMPS (IN THE MAGNETIC CITY)

> I fell in love with machines.
> I built my own electronics.
> My father was a piano.
> **Rock musician heard on the radio**

The Lewisite method is obsessed with the identification of a technological being. Lewis believed that modern society was a test tube, with power-mad doctors and clinics named Hitler, Stalin, Wall Street, Bloomsbury, and Hollywood accelerating evolution to create the perfect social cog: weak, malleable, unimaginative—a devourer, not a creator.

The twentieth century ran on a principle of total transformation. Humanity itself would be adapted to appropriate technology. Soon it would be hard to tell the robots from the people.

A quick survey of this process of identification: it starts in *Tarr* (1918). Otto Kreisler, the German artist who focuses the novel's action, is not human. He is Auto Chrysler, an automaton bent on self-obliteration. "The origin of the comic," Lewis commented, "is in a machine trying to act like a man." We add: the origin of the tragic may be in a person trying to become a machine. Kreisler severs physical connections; he smashes into people; he has transformed himself into a robot.

In an exchange near the end of the novel, the protagonist, Tarr, explains the transformation from man into machine or superbeing. "You are my efficient chimpanzee then for keeps?" Kreisler's pregnant lover asks Tarr.

"No, I'm the new animal; we haven't thought up a name
for him yet—the thing that will succeed the superman."

Tarr is an animal, "a wild body": he is a r-rat, spelled backwards with a stutter. Tarr is the intellectual-artist: he observes; he argues; he comments. Lewis's emphasis on visual detail renders the novel-essay's rhythm flat, until Auto Chrysler drives over Tarr, as it were, onto the scene. Kreisler is a precursor of the storm trooper: he is a nobody who is dangerous because he motors on brutality.

In *The Apes of God* (1930), Bloomsbury becomes the diabolical lab of the inauthentic self. Here the efficient chimps have taken over the social machinery. Bloomsbury is the scene of "restless machines" acting like people, of puppets and phonies running unchecked. Apes imitate life. They steal passion from the true spirits and then trivialize the art experience. In these "essays in a new human mathematic", everyone is an artist: but if everyone is an artist, then there can be no art. The unique has been squashed by a production-line of apes and fakes. The only true artist, Horace Zagreus (his name an echo of the satirist, Horace), is a windy (talkative) outsider. He guides his innocent Dante, Daniel Boleyn, through the inferno, and points out specimens while lecturing on satire: "Next week I will accompany you myself to several choice places...."

Lewis was typically and perversely ambivalent about this separation of the human from the anti-human. He tried to be an unprecedented figure in modernist letters: hence his pursuit of an outlaw's code. He would be a sneak and a spy, quick with his talent to dodge the returning volleys. He wanted to flush out his public into the open where a showdown would be witnessed. "You know Baudelaire's fable of the obsequious vagabond, cringing for alms?" Tarr explains. "For all reply the poet seizes a heavy stick and lays about the beggar with it. When he is almost battered to pieces...he rises up and falls upon the poet tooth and nail....The poet is enchanted: he has accomplished something!" Yet Lewis discovered that if no one comes out in public to retaliate, it may be because there is no longer anyone there.

But how does a government, a corporation, a literary club, or any institution conspire ("con-spire": to breathe together) to rob the Plain Reader of his ability to breathe freely? How does massification work?

The power doctors leave you helpless, afraid, and dependent on them. They wish to turn you (us) into a baby.

To grow up, to do what Peter Pan so wisely refrained from doing, is to think and struggle; and all thinking is evil and struggle is useless. Give up your will; cease to think for yourself; regard your employer as your good, kind father or uncle; leave everything in his hands. *(The Art of Being Ruled)*

The above quote may be the first use of Peter Pan to denote the child-man who will not accept responsibility for his actions. This child-man is a technological tool, another result of the flattening process of the Childish-mass.

Throughout *The Art of Being Ruled, Paleface, Time and Western Man,* and *Men Without Art,* Lewis expands his tableaux of the mechanized society. He sees

— the disintegration of the family unit
— the cult of the child (the Peter Pans)
— doctrinaire dilettantism
— the war on the intellect

And he adds to his zoo of puppets, "cranks", and "pseudoists"

— the erotic child cult (sex and youth obsession)
— musicalization (oral culture)
— the romance of extremism
— the diminishing of the word

There is some foresight here. During this period Lewis reads as if he is describing contemporary North American society (downtown Toronto on a Saturday night?), and not the test tubes he studied in Bloomsbury and continental Europe.

If the art of being ruled is the art of not being fooled, Lewis's presumption is that power can successfully work us over. If the Lewisite method is "ju-jitsu for the governed", who are the governors? Despite his metaphoric precision at describing effect, he is less specific at naming the cause. This is because in the modern age Lewis felt that the causes were invisible: they formed "a concealed will".

Power cells like Wall Street (in our terms IBM or the IMF) could control the social mood, the mind of a time, and ruin people without appearing to do so directly. They operated through ambiguity. They moved in backstages. "It is, in fact, quite surprising how totalitarian you can be without anybody so much as guessing that they are a whit less free than they were before," Lewis commented.

So to locate the secretive sources, the reader and writer became hunters together. The investigations would lead down into the cultural capitals (London, Venice, Paris, New York, Toronto), where "capital rules", through the parties and studios, "the clubs and pubs". We are asked to look at billboards, newspapers, movies, and advertisements and to record the outward signs, the languages of the cabals and trusts. In the rush of crowds we could study effect and affectation. Fashion and styles, whether in literature or clothing, could sweep the citizen up and collect him into campaigns called Age, Sex, Identity, Youth, and Nationalism.

And the name of the twentieth-century drug? Speed.

Dynamical, as the most 'hurried' man is aware, means the bustle and rush of action—of Big Business, Armaments, Atlantic hops, Wall Street, and Mussolini....

With this speed, there is a rhythm.

An automatic and stereotyped rhythm is what most people desire for themselves...but consciousness and possession of the self is not compatible with a set rhythm.

In another era, that rhythm would be called conformity.

The Enemy's sensitivity to power made him palpably aware of mass influence; he seems to have felt it around him, like something clutching and gagging him. He knew that the way to control people was to degrade them: make them feel squeezed and small, lower than Kafka's insect. He knew modern society had the power through advertising and "Press Terrorism", in monopolies of communication networks, to inflate an individual's image into meaningless celebrity, letting that person briefly soar like a hot-air balloon.

His expert diagnoses of power manifestations may have come in part because he was excessively sensitive to physical touch. He invariably describes being in a crowd as a form of suicide. Also note the projective style of his prose. His word choice can be aggressive to the point of irritation: the reader is never allowed to relax. But because Lewis felt closed in by others, he was always lashing out. The air he breathed was choked with *Zeitgeist* furies that threatened to drain his vitality. Once he forged himself into the demolition device portrayed in his 1921 self-portrait (*The Tyro*), he spent the decades between the wars warning his readers to take precautions against "air pollution", to beware of "machines acting like people", and not to be susceptible to hypnotic instruction.

It is not new, of course, for us to hear that Soviet and fascist societies are experimental labs with a new being as their desired result. Czeslaw Milosz's *The Captive Mind* (English edition, 1953) describes such a state from the view of one caught in the squeeze between the Soviet Imperium and the Nazi Empire. The choices are clear when the opposition is a tank. What was new about Lewis's idea was his perception that the West had manufactured its own peculiar type: the soulless consumer. In the 1920s and '30s Lewis observed this processing being enacted with blind enthusiasm; he saw more sophisticated ways of murdering "freedom and delight". All the reshaping would go on with subtle efficiency; all this would go on unseen. And we would feed ourselves to the body politic unaware that something deadly had slipped into our midst.

COSMIC MAN

You ain't gonna make a monkey out of me!
James Cagney, in *Public Enemy*

Against the efficient chimps who ape real life, in the 1940s Lewis promoted an alternative: the Cosmic Man, released from nationalism and roots, agile enough to slip from under oppression and depression, adept with discovery and disguise; a chameleon, at home in the world community.

The Cosmic Man, however, appears in the lesser-known books Lewis wrote for a quick advance. He believed that technology could give individuals the flexibility of change. Don't dismantle the machines, he implied: question them and deal with them. The ideal state is one in which varieties of characters can coexist without imposing on one another. Leadership in "the melting pot" could be provided by the officials of the Flood: intellectuals "sharp as razors", informed citizens, and well-trained politicians.

The shock is that Lewis's society of cosmic people, described in *America and Cosmic Man*, is similar to the pluralism of the North American liberal democracies. This supposed supporter of dictators dreamed of a political-social system that would not destroy creative personality. America was his prototype of potential, a society in contact with the frontier, where identity could be shed like a withered skin, vitality refreshed, and European tragedies forgotten.

America was for him a whole nation of outlaws. "America may be regarded as solitary...."; and "...with a great appetite for nonsense." Here was proof that a state could be a benign mechanism: "their techniques race ahead, leaping into the future." The cosmo (politan) person is loyal to global conditions. "I am quite serious when I say that this is what heaven must be like...a rootless, irresponsible city...where the spirit is released from all too-close contacts with other people....But where everything is superficially fraternal...."

Lewis found readers, but no public, in an America he had idealized. In Canada, the other new land, he found only silence. He returned to London after World War II where he resumed his chronicling of "the dance of the Dark Forces of Unreason". He said (in 1954): "What every artist should try to prevent is...the exhibitionist extremist promoter driving the whole bag of tricks [civilization] into a nihilistic nothingness or zero."

Note: the word "zero" is repeated with ominous regularity in his last books.

FROM THE LIBRARY

Lewis says in *The Art of Being Ruled*

Many great writers...address audiences who do not exist....To address passionately and sometimes with very great wisdom *people who do not exist* has this advantage...that there will always be a group of people who, seeing a man shouting apparently at somebody or other, and seeing nobody else in sight, will think it is they who are being addressed...

The old books I signed out from the library were crammed with marginalia. Clearly, some readers felt it was they who were being addressed by Lewis.

I had felt that scribbling in a rare edition was like criminal defacement. But suddenly I recognized the hand of one note taker. And I soon began to watch for the remarks in the margins.

The marginal notes in *The Writer and the Absolute* and other works revealed another author's early routes: in those out-of-print books, the comments responded to the call on the page; that slow hand with its left-handed scrawl showed the seed of future thinking, a growth leading to the application of Lewis's method to the psychic effects of television and telephones and a Magnetic City charged with acceleration and amplification.

> now that the earth has become one big village, with telephones laid on from one end to the other, and air transport, both speedy and safe....

In the left-hand corner, I found this faded phrase in pencil

> a global village

The handwriting belonged to Marshall McLuhan. The book: *America and Cosmic Man*, a first edition, 1948.

SPIRITS OF THE AIR

In the 1950s, after Lewis had gone blind rather than let emergency surgery interfere with the operation of his mind, he worked to complete *The Human Age* trilogy. Volume I, *The Childermass*, had been published in 1928 with the proviso "to be continued". More than twenty-five years later (1955), *Monstre Gai* and *Malign Fiesta* carried on the portrait of the Magnetic City after death.

Satire meets metaphysics in these novels. Lewis's stylistic fireworks have been subdued: his voice is conversational, more in tune with the essays of the 1950s than his puppet fiction of the 1920s. He writes with knowledge of the implications of a thermonuclear holocaust and of supertechnology. Here existence has been reduced to parties and parades and controversies between dead souls, angels, and devils.

> This was not life at all, but something artificial, in which the values of life-on-earth were dressed up in a different way, and manifested themselves with clarity....
> *(Monstre Gai)*

The Human Age title is at once ironic and a lament for a life that has passed. Humanity was "frail, puny, shortlived, ridiculous, but...*preferable*". In this post-life, no one can be trusted and no one is safe from control. "Man undisciplined and in the rough was not at all popular with the angelic overlord."

Matapolis and Third City are strange environs that resemble welfare settlements designed by a bored Expressionist. *The Human Age*, however, is not a sequential series of Newtonian boxes named hell, purgatory, and heaven: it is "a valueless vacuum". All is in a condition of complete uncertainty.

> ...before the modern age, yes, back in the Age of Faith, there was a Heaven and there was a Hell....Things have progressed as they have down on earth...great changes...have taken place. As we all know, and can see for ourselves, the *Good* and the *Bad* are blurred....We no longer see things in stark black and

white....What was once the Devil (to whom one "sold one's soul" and so forth) well today, he is a very unconvinced devil, and our Padishah...is a very unconvinced Angel. *(Monstre Gai)*

The Human Age is not truly science fiction. It is a visionary's map of Lewis's intuition of the possible effect of electric communication networks on individual integrity.

Man [Satan–Sammael explains] is acquiring a technological magic which may in the end equal us in resource....

The robots have vanished from Lewis's canvas. His metaphors are no longer machine-like: they are bodiless and sexless. Ghosts speak to ghosts; directives are issued from above; life is automated by programmers no one sees; the rulers have disappeared, and only hollow frontmen are left. There is no ground of reality and therefore no choice. Warfare is rampant; everyone is in the air; rumour has replaced information; and an overloaded passivity is encouraged. Anyone with any character is perceived to be a monster, a demon, like a mythic reminder of the past.

Lewis wrote his manuscripts for performance on the radio: over the air. The show was produced and recorded by D.G. Bridson for the BBC Third Programme in 1955. The novels were published in that same year. The reviews compared *The Human Age* favourably to Swift, and spoke of the author's misanthropy.

In a condemned flat, the blind man listened to the acoustic future: the spirits of the air. That airing predated the arrival of a generation who would receive their news from TV screens and hi-fi speakers, but who would not be the readers he had worked to provoke and protect.

3

THE ART OF SELF-DESTRUCTION

"I gave a book to Lewis to sign," McLuhan said. "We were standing near a place where there was an incinerator....He took it. [pause] Glanced at the title. And without a word ripped it up...and tossed the pages into the incinerator....That book was *Hitler*. [softly] He just stood and watched it burn."

Hitler (1931) haunts Lewis's reputation. It was the work that almost finished Lewis's hope of playing a prominent part in his place; and it calls into question the ability of artists to immunize themselves against the infections of their time.

"Diabolical," McLuhan said. "Lewis felt there was something...diabolical about that book....He hated to talk about it."

To incinerate your work is a desperate gesture; it can also be a recognition of a mistake. Lewis knew he had been mesmerized by "an immense indignant thought". So if we are to recall him as a cartographer of the mass-age, then

we must enter the dark alleys where the eye can be fooled
and voices can betray.

We know Lewis had rejected a test-tube approach to politics. But, he had wondered, what is an alternative line of
credit for social reorganization? Capitalism was a failure,
because cruelty and humiliation typified the conditions
of depression and inflation. Lewis feared the effects of
monopolies and corporation states in the West. Marxist
dialectics, he thought, would produce an economic robot
without personality or imagination. Thus if invisible credit
and monopoly determine who prospers and this occurs
beyond the citizen's view, it could take a strong person to
reform values. Lewis did not believe a state had to be vi-
cious. Political power could be channelled for enlightened
purposes. "A Vorticist King! Why Not?"

What critics miss about *Hitler* was that it was published before the brutal National-Socialist agenda was
launched (1933). What those critics also misunderstand
is that *Hitler* misapplies Lewis's own method of perception. The elements are there: city (environment); historical
figure; book; diagnosis; prognosis.

For Lewis, political force was focused in the "hypnotic
eye" of Hitler. Lewis was attracted to clear purpose, hard
line, and discipline. For this occasion, he went inside the
Zeitgeist: he stood too close to the moment.

> In the following articles [he writes] it is as an exponent—
> not as critic nor yet as advocate of German National-
> socialism, or Hitlerism, that I come forward....an un-
> prejudiced and fairly detailed account of this great and
> novel factor in world affairs should be at the disposal of
> the intelligent Anglo-Saxon.

He begins in Berlin, "the dazzling boulevard world", "the pervert's paradise". Cities are enticing centres: they can seduce the critical "I". Thus the urban ground, Berlin, is reviewed with sightseeing eyes.

In Lewis's mind a fiction unfolded. Hitler was Otto Kreisler with a mind: he was energy and will joined with leadership. Hitler is visualized as a hostile opponent to his decaying society. He would arrest the decadence of his Magnetic City, and the crash of the German economy would be halted. But Lewis refused to push his impressions through to a critique of the Nazi vortex. He shut himself to Hitler's evil. He wanted to stay untouched ("indifferent, paring his fingernails...."); he became the man in the iron mask, cold, abstract, absorbing the drama of death.

Lewis's satirical method moves to exaggeration (blow things up). When he treats Hitler's anti-Semitism, he is cavalier. " 'For better or worse,' in the words of the English marriage service, there is the Jew! Feminine, and in many ways very unpleasant—all people have their bad sides...." These witless remarks leave Lewis open to many charges; primarily, we find a failure to imagine the effect of his statements. There is more: "Hitler himself—once he had obtained power—would show increasing moderation and tolerance." Lewis's reviewer's tone turns uneasy with *Mein Kampf*. He points out the Hitlerite emphasis on race, blood, and tribe: "race loyalty is one of the elementary conditions of self-security." Hitler's nationalism, he explains, is based on historical roots, a reclaiming of German traditions and borders. He analyses the Social Credit economic theory in Hitler's manifesto ("the credit cranks") and concludes that "the fall of Europe...is the result...of an enormous new factor—machinery and industrial technique."

Lewis reads intellectually, without feeling or intuition, and so cannot hear Hitler's hate. He turns a blind "I" and ignores the frenzy. This occurs because Lewis understood the urge to smash his opponents: the power to possess and dominate, like the sense of being dispossessed (without a role), is his underlying fixation.

> It may have been because this very complex and sensitive man was so responsive to the claims of violence—because he made it so much his own—that he understood its opposite as well as he did. The notion of domination, and of the struggle for domination, obsessed him. But he was also obsessed by those refinements of the intellect which cannot co-exist with the struggle for existence. ...He was an extremist, and extremes meet. (*The Hitler Cult And How It Will End*, 1939)

This is Lewis on Nietzsche. The statement is naked autobiography, the closest that Lewis came to direct confession.

He misperceived Hitler's power ("a puppet thrown up in response to an intolerable internal situation") because he could not envisage the implications of the Nazi program. Once Hitler's "talent" to organize the economy was translated into military action, the energy became blitzkrieg—and the suicide of a nation. What perplexes readers is how Lewis could not see that Hitler could only control the critical "I" by obliterating individual conscience. Here was a lab-man turning citizens into butchers and vermin.

But the seductions of Nazism were like the allure of a new sleek machine. Many were caught up in the sensation of the superstate and the invasion of unreason.

From the *New English Weekly*, March 21, 1940. The author: George Orwell. The subject: *Mein Kampf*.

I should like to put it on record that I have never been able to dislike Hitler. Ever since he came to power— till then like nearly everyone I had been deceived into thinking that he did not matter—I have reflected that I would certainly kill him if I could get within reach of him, but that I could feel no personal animosity. The fact is that there is something deeply appealing about him. One feels it again when one sees his photographs— and I recommend especially the photograph at the beginning of Hurst and Blackett's edition, which shows Hitler in his early Brownshirt days. It is a pathetic, dog-like face, the face of a man suffering under intolerable wrongs....He is the martyr, the self-sacrificing hero who fights single-handed against impossible odds....One feels, as with Napoleon, that he is fighting against destiny, that he *can't* win, and yet that he somehow deserved to....

...And he [Hitler] has grasped the falsity of the hedonistic attitude to life. Nearly all western thought since the last war, certainly all "progressive" thought, has assumed tacitly that human beings desire nothing beyond ease, security, and avoidance of pain....Hitler...knows that human beings *don't* only want comfort, safety, short working-hours, hygiene, birth control, and, in general, common sense: they also, at least intermittently, want struggle and self-sacrifice, not to mention drums, flags, and loyalty parades. However they may be as economic theories, Fascism and Nazism are psychologically far sounder than any hedonistic conception of life....Whereas Socialism, and even capitalism in a more grudging way have said to the people "I offer you a good time," Hitler has said to them "I offer you struggle, danger, and death," and as a result a whole nation flings itself at his feet....

It is too late to point a disapproving finger. Orwell shows how deep the psychological pull of Nazism had gone and how Hitler had penetrated into the mass psyche. That attraction was so effective that Orwell, who was irreproachably anti-Nazi, was not immune. And Lewis, who could not stop up his senses to the flow of radioactive history, participated in the same conspiracy of seduction.

Yet it does not seem to help to insist that by 1939 Lewis had written *The Hitler Cult and How It Will End*, a caveat on Nazi barbarism. "Hitler is a 'villain' who, if he is not sufficiently hissed, becomes really dangerous....So hiss! as you value your life." It seems to do no good to say that by 1940 Lewis had banished himself to Canada to protest "the spectacle of the European suicide". Nor does it help to recall that D.H. Lawrence, Pound, and William Butler Yeats respected fascism. It is Lewis who is relentlessly chastized for succumbing to the Hitlerite Time Ghost. In John Harrison's *The Reactionaries* (1966), Lewis is treated with disgust and cast aside. The best scholarly study of Lewis is Fredric Jameson's *Fables of Aggression: The Modernist as Fascist*, a book written from a Marxist-psychoanalytical perspective. To simplify Jameson's subtle argument: he posits that Lewis's style and thought are inherently fascistic because of his hatred of levelling "proletarianization", his belief in classical authority and elitism, and his racist stereotyping and muscled prose. This complex thesis ignores Lewis's nonfiction recantations and his dream of the Cosmic Man who is undogmatic, responsive, and free.

The second indictment: *The Jews: Are They Human?* (1939). The title stops us cold. In this pamphlet, "the duellist" fired a salvo at what he sensed, correctly, was a prevailing wind: anti-Semitism. "...because Germany,

Hungary, Italy, Poland, Czechoslovakia," he writes, "and other countries are freezing out their Jewish minorities." But why produce a pamphlet with a title certain to provoke revulsion? Lewis answers

> The Jews are the "human beings" *par excellence.* Perhaps that is the proper answer to the present question....I shall make out a case for their humanity in these pages. Consequently the antisemite may throw this book to the other side of the room.

In the Foreword, Lewis checks his sarcasm. He is condescending (he was with everybody; he never played favourites), but no savaging of his target follows.

The Jews: Are They Human? is not a profound book, nor is it anti-Semitic. Like Pound and Eliot, Lewis identified "the big abstract money spinners" with Jewish bankers and families (the Rothschilds). But he parts with race contempt. His book is, of all things, an urgent plea for restraint: to desist "the black crimes" of "Christian-inspired" hatred of Jews. "We have a lot to answer for," he admits. His polemic is intended as a warning against genocidal impulses and the anti-human policies of the totalitarian regimes. "Let us understand ourselves, as well as the Jews, if we can, and realize that the only course we *can* take, being what we are, is the humane one." Jewish bankers were a part of the same capitalist system that debases everyone. "In many ways the Jew is too honest, too direct," he says; "his misdemeanours in the commercial world are largely a myth."

His critique pounces on Jewish nationalism. His dislike of the crowd mentality makes him uncomfortable with religious insularity. But the tribalism is what insures the Jews of "a rough ride". Lewis acknowledges that the Jews' toughness allowed their communities to endure. He declares that in his "enlightened" vision of the

Cosmic Man, the Jewish stereotype is "out of date", like the British John Bull. Again Lewis attacks cliché—the mechanical response to something real. He offers a new deal in his conclusion and sounds like a literary Franklin Roosevelt. (Roosevelt would be his model of the good ruler in *America and Cosmic Man*.)

Lewis advocates admitting the Jewish refugees from Europe into England. He demands that the English forget the myth of the Jews "with the mark of Cain". Lewis has been likened to a cerebral Céline, but there is no trace here of the scatalogical disgust and homicidal raving found in Dr. Destouches's *L'Ecole des cadavres* (1936). Nor do we find the anti-Semitic rants of Pound's pre-World War II polemics on economics or his deranged Rome radio speeches. When Lewis writes a badly constructed phrase like "The anglo-saxons and other Europeans should reform ourselves: by so doing we should be liquidating the 'Jewish Problem'," we cringe from our distance. But what he meant by the "Jewish Problem" was anti-Semitism itself. Lewis felt that every attitude must be examined because the twentieth century had to be rethought and reimagined.

> But we must do something more active than just not go back. We must make up for the doings of the so-called "Christians" of yesterday—who degraded the Jew, and then mocked him for being degraded....Let us for Heaven's sake make an end of this silly nightmare....

Lewis was making amends for *Hitler*. And he was trying to overturn the murderous mood in Europe that he may have felt in part responsible for.

But this does not explain the masochistic guilt implicit in his self-defeating title. He describes himself as an outsider: "like the Jews," he says. *The Jews: Are They*

Human? masks the true question: *Wyndham Lewis, Is He Human Too?* It reveals his estrangement from popular (and self?) respect. He may have been making a case for his own humanity; and he may have had premonitions of something darker to come, when the proficient machinery of the camps would feed on "the human beings *par excellence*".

Yet the poisoned memory of The Enemy lingers.

NATURE MORTE

If it moves, shoot it. If it doesn't, paint it.
SAC standing orders

The Art of Being Ruled developed from Lewis's skills as a painter, and the emphasis in that work from 1926 is on art. His method tries to arrest the viewer and still time. But since you cannot stop speed—for time is money—you would have to promote other techniques for maintaining a point of view.

"I am for the wisdom of the Eye, rather than that of the Ear," Lewis said. To counter the onslaught of time (flux, fatalism, crowds, and emotion), which he called "the Ear culture", he would step up "the Eye" (analysis, coolness, solitude, distance).

Clarity is impossible when events rush by. Speed makes experience a blur or a hum. The result: anxiety, intolerance. So how do you call a halt? Stand still.

Nature morte a still life is called in French. Translation: Dead nature.

Death is the thing [Tarr explains] that differentiates art and life. Art is identical with the idea of permanence. Art

is a continuity and not an individual spasm: but life is the
idea of a person....Deadness is the first condition for
art: the second is the absence of soul, in the human and
sentimental sense. With a statue its lines and masses
are its soul...it has *no inside*....

Tarr and *The Apes of God* are pictorial displays
punctuated by dialogue: they are static tableaux with
critical commentaries. When Lewis tells a story, as in *Self-
Condemned*, he returns to plot and character. *Time and
Western Man* does not have an argument formed from a
stated thesis and building towards a conclusion. Subjects
are studied like paintings in a gallery, frozen portraits in
the artist's mind.

Thus *The Apes of God* is among the first modernist
anti-books. It is utterly unreadable for most people. Lewis
worked against the reader's inclination to go forward.
Prose needs pacing. And pictorialism in fiction suppresses
the narrative flow. "The wisdom of the Eye" (excessive
emphasis on the visual) cut Lewis off from common sense,
all the senses moving in consort.

We suddenly see how the reader becomes both Lewis's
partner and his victim. The size of *The Apes of God*
signalled Lewis's perverse intentions: the editions were
so large that they could not be comfortably held. (Eliot's
comment: "so massive I have no words for it.")

In the 1920s and '30s, Lewis used a style that con-
tradicted his energy. He had said, "the greatest satire is
non-moral," by which he meant that you do not moral-
ize with your targets; but his aim was moral. He despised
convulsion. Yet his thinking and feeling responded to
breakdown. His style is adaptable to fragment, mosaic,
aphorism. And so, paradoxically, linear attempts to deal
with his *oeuvre* are doomed. Again the intellectual pressure of Nietzsche is concealed behind Lewis's exposés and

explorations of superism, the intellectual presence he argued with and refuted. Like Nietzsche, Lewis's talent for self-annihilation was boundless.

Lewis is not the first writer to lunge at the "*hypocrite lecteur*". But when he turned his passion outward to assault his public, he strangled the humanity out of his work: the satirist as godlike destroyer of sympathy. The Lewisite voice was summarily rejected; "...they hate my tone," he said.

VOCATION OF TERROR

We come to the question of the voice that whips and herds the reader.

"This annihilatory punishment...was so fearful and dreadful that no one could resist it." Elias Canetti described the effect of hearing Karl Kraus's voice at a lecture in Vienna in 1924, the year that *The Apes of God* was serialized in *Criterion*. "Every verdict was carried out on the spot. Once pronounced, it was irrevocable. We all witnessed the execution...."

In *The Conscience of Words* (German: 1968; English: 1979), Canetti asks what influence a writer's words can have on the reader's mind. He concludes there can be murder in the tone and intent. When the word can kill, it is then that an author can turn author-itarian.

What happens when killing is the intent of a voice? For the vocation of terror to proceed, the apes in a supernatural zoo cannot be real. The author writes without a conscience: the prey become abstract stereotypes, figments from a dream, fragments from "an intoxicated hallucination" of automata, puppets, and dolls.

Lewis wanted to separate killers from creators through his polemics and art. At a point in his word frenzy, however, he became an assassin. This occurs in *The Apes of God*, *The Doom of Youth*, and *The Art of Being Ruled*, when his prose turns deadly, like a discharge of loathing and contempt. It has been said that you cannot understand evil until you have had the desire to kill either someone else or yourself. Lewis was a professional cynic who bullied his victims (among them the Sitwells) because he doubted their right to "a paltry existence". He knew that, in spite of praise from peers, some excellent press, and controversy, his books did not sell. His audience was highbrow, composed of artists, like Roy Campbell, and quarries, like Virginia Woolf. (Note: "Why do I shrink from reading W.L.?" Woolf asks in a 1924 entry in *A Writer's Diary*, after exposure to the *Criterion* excerpt from *Apes*. And later: "The W.L. disease lasted only two days....") To reform the decayed values of the West, most of the old had to be wiped out. But if all things are doubted, eventually nothing is left. For the artist for whom art means "the hard, the cold, the mechanical, the static", and for whom words were agents of "the clean slate", the world soon becomes "a zero", "a city in a plain" where there are no humane options.

Canetti tells us why a first-class intellectual would speak in a voice of relentless enmity.

> I cannot imagine a writer who was not controlled and paralyzed by someone else's authenticity at an early time. In the humiliation of his rape, when he feels that there is nothing of his own, that he is not himself, does not know what he himself is, his concealed powers begin to stir. His personality articulates itself, arising from the resistance....("Karl Kraus: The School of Resistance")

Substitute reader for writer in the quote above. Then we can glimpse why the gifted Lewis seemed to slam against his interests.

In World War I, the "Boches" were "them": the enemy, a slogan repeated to the troops sent to the trenches to save civilization and die. Lewis called himself The Enemy in 1927 and recalled barbed wire, machine guns, and *zeit*-gas for the Lost Generation. He made himself the threat. He meant we are the enemy; the infection is within.

Lewis set out to stiffen his readers' resistance to propaganda and coercion. He made his devil's-advocate persona strong to make us strong. A writer may say "No, I won't add to the darkness of my age"; but if you want to shock the public out of its moral sleep, you may not be able to avoid responsibility for a negative result when it wakes up. Lewis demanded independence: his and ours. (His deathbed remark: "Mind your own business.") The Plain Reader should therefore stir against every destroyer, including the one who wore the mask of The Enemy.

Lewis defined sentimentality as a refusal to carry emotions and ideas through to their extreme. He was honest enough to extend his assassin streak even if that meant condemning himself. And it did. He said: the face people see in satire's mirror is seldom their own. In *The Revenge for Love* and *Self-Condemned*, the principal players are named Percy Hardcastle and René Harding. Each character ends exiled, in a cell, in "a cemetery of shells"; each has a momentary revelation when he sees that he has been the cause of someone's death; each is left desolate in his loneliness. The repeated "hard" in the names of those who are stand-ins for P. Wind-Damn Lewis shows the vocation of terror consuming its last victim. "We all play those tricks that make the angels weep," he said.

He was unsparingly hard on everyone.

LEWISITE

I am no man, I am dynamite.
Nietzsche

Lewis (def.): an iron dove-tailed tendon that is made in sections, used in hoisting large stones.

Lewis Gun: a gas operated, air-cooled machine gun fed by a drum magazine and first used in World War I.

Lewisite: developed as a nerve gas during World War I but never used.

Blast: a word stemming from the Anglo-Saxon *blaest*, meaning a blowing (wind), linked to breath, breathe, and blaze. An English slang outburst: "Oh, blast it." Also a detonation, a gust, a wreck. In North American slang: "What a blast, man," or "like y'know…I was blasted" (i.e., a state of mind wasted).

Hitler did the first damage to his name. Thereafter critics and publishers began to shun him. ("Meanwhile, back here in London, my book was being spat at.…") Two of his realistic novels, *The Revenge for Love* (1937) and *The Vulgar Streak* (1941), were written when his reputation was low. Both may be read as indirect commentaries on running with ideological packs rather than against, on how unseen forces can devastate the self. (Note: after 1939, Lewis did not call himself The Enemy again.)

If we return to the odious *Hitler*, we find surprising, quiet asides where Lewis dreams of "a Golden Age". He had the desire to go "beyond action and reaction" to classical serenity, "leisure and abundance".

An outlaw claims to be above the law.

Lewis challenged his era and tried to instruct the Plain Reader on how to transcend the times. He made an effort not to be fooled by supermen and then wished to be one himself. He fired out book after book, polemic after polemic, to arrest the drive of death in western society.

"I can see all the dead," he said on the eve of World War II, when he realized another war was imminent; "…I would like to say to those bereaved and helpless masses, if I could reach them: Count your Dead! I would take each one aside and shout: They are alive! Can't you see that they are not dead yet?"

Editions of *Hitler* are hard to find. Most libraries don't carry it.

Lewis threw McLuhan's copy into the fire and performed a self-critical act. Then he stood silently and watched while a historical memory burned.

4

NOW

The picture today: there are few battlefields with trenches and troops. The view is cloudy and polluted. Magnetic Cities dominate the globe. The Forward Observation Posts are at extreme risk. Wholesale slaughter impends. Words often seem to be sent telegraphically, as if over teletype, for immediate attention. Thinking requires effort. Books are consumed between subway stops, during jet stopovers, between telephone calls, before sleep. Words tend to get garbled in the incomplete transmissions, and translators are in short supply.

What would Lewis say about this state?

What could he say?

The Plain Reader outside academia may have no way of understanding his range and rage. It may be impossible to fully retrieve Lewis. To deal with him would require a comprehensive intimacy with Spengler, Proudhon, Sorel, Joyce, Benda, Shaw, Proust, and (of all people) Anita Loos. And we have entered what Milan Kundera says is "the elementary state of music (music minus thought)".

The Lost Generation became the Beat Generation, which became the Me Generation, which became the Pepsi Generation. This New Wave may be the first truly Sound Generation, raised without a context of literacy.

Moreover, the education system that I myself went through virtually discouraged books. I grew up out of balance, with amplified guitars, radios, records, and a TV addiction. The musical milieu I knew has produced passionate voices; dance, theatre, and film are truly the arts of our time. Nevertheless, our society now seems to urge us not to think, to be submissive and self-absorbed, to go with the flow of consumerism. Concentration is constantly shattered; the word is processed; and ours may already be the anti-book world that Lewis anticipated.

SOLITARY OUTWIT

You can't expect people to pay you for enjoying yourself!
Pound to Lewis

Yet when I return to Lewis's writings, I find pleasure in his outmoded demand for truth and in his reckless wrecking of the status quo in literature, politics, and philosophy. "Laughter is the Wild Body's Song of Triumph. ...Laughter is the bark of delight of a gregarious animal at the proximity of its kind," he said. "Bless the Solitude of Laughter." If you can laugh, you can breathe. And if you can breathe, then you are not finished yet.

Lest we forget, Lewis was drunk "with the laughing gas of the abyss." Against the Magnetic City, he advocated wit. "Human life could not be serious if it tried...." Against the efficient chimps, try mental agility. "Cherish and develop, side by side, your six most constant

indications of different personalities." Unpredictability insures human endurance. "Each trench must have another
one behind it." When society runs too smoothly, there
is the danger that we will be smoothed over. "Admit-
tedly I approach the human problem with no heroical nor
sentimental design. But the cheapjack political journalist...must not be allowed to get away with the charge
that I preach a power doctrine...that I offer to the would-
be tyrant a tempting prospect of man's helplessness."
Outside, the air is cool and free.

Lewis's philosophy of the outside is a manifesto of
mind restoration and preparation, of laughter and remembering. Which is why he has been mislabelled a
conservative. Labelling is a way of killing a live thing.
And the Lewisite method is meant to outwit the specialist.
"We fight first on one side, then on the other," he said in
Blast. Later, in a letter, he said: "[I am] partly communist
and partly fascist, with a distinct streak of monarchism in
my marxism, but at bottom anarchist with a healthy passion for order." Or: a left-wing, right-wing, conservative,
radical, nihilist. His thinking tried to balance opposites in
a rational equilibrium without resorting to an ideological
hard line.

Lewis certainly chose to preserve his Plain Reader
from an almost inhuman detachment. And his attempt to
stop the destructive tide of his time ("Wind 'em," Pound
called his friend who kept watch) ended in the misin-
terpretation of him as a man devoured by hate. Another
paradox: many books by this author who preferred the
timeless and stationary have dated. We cannot comprehend his polemics without reference to the 1920s and '30s
and the reputations (like the Sitwells) that belong to the
period. Most of his novels and essays never achieve a for-
mal unity: they are rambling, repetitive, digressive. But I
repeat that there is value in his provocation training. "He
who opens his eyes wide enough will always find himself

alone." Lewis strained to snatch back, from the ephemeral and the dictatorial, a critical identity, a singular wit.

A sense of humour may not be enough to outwit political domination; laughter cannot overthrow the tyranny of inarticulacy. A good nature will not relieve the realities of privation and pain. But Lewis thought that wit was the flash of spirit, a rebellion against the iron bars of the powerhouse. His writings have too often suffered from those who do not share his savage smile. He said: "I have never been to a funeral, but a desire to laugh is supposed to obsess people on such occasions.....It seems so terribly absurd—or so absurdly terrible."

Wit is permanently out of place: it is your first offence and your last line of defence. Wit understands that the inability to play is surely a sign of madness. Wit is the centre of character that keeps you in balance when you set out to put others off balance.

> Still I hope I may have entertained you, here and there, for it is amazing the number of different sorts of things I have done. And I hope that, in addition to the entertainment—as my sight is keen, as nothing escapes my eye, and as I may claim a respectable measure of common sense...it may be that, in this amusing way by following my body round, as we have done, some portion of my experience may have passed over into you. (*Blasting and Bombardiering*)

5

STILL IN THE RUIN

Reports of Lewis's years in post-World War II London (courtesy of eyewitnesses Eliot, D.G. Bridson, and Hugh Kenner), confirm that his mood had turned sombre. In the Preface to a reissued *Apes of God*, he remarked that his early work had been too lighthearted. The emotion is understandable. He had spent his working life mostly in poverty and in writing self-cancelling throwaways.

Yet in the unfinished fourth volume of *The Human Age*, titled *The Trial of Man*, he was willing to re-evaluate his thinking and add a paradise to his human comedy. Ruthless self-analysis was his key to renewal. He moved toward a spiritual resolution: "mankind matters...." God would appear: "...something which was not zero."

He still searched for calm and coherence in the twentieth-century storm. But paradise was beyond him. A portrait of Wyndham Lewis must be a portrait of a fight against chaos.

He interrupted his major effort, and—with his genius for disturbance—wrote a Graham Greene-like thriller, *The*

Red Priest (1956). While Pound published his "Rock-Drill Cantos" when he was in the St. Elizabeth's asylum, and Eliot contemplated his Nobel Prize (received in 1948), Lewis tried to produce a best seller that would influence the flux of post-war events and restore his public reputation. The potboiler has only one memorable passage: the concluding one. In it the exiled couple with the absurd name of Tertullian give birth to a child, Zero. "Like his terrible father," the novel concludes, "fated to blast his way across space and time." It is a final sentence pronounced on himself. The statement is riddled with self-referential puns on every Lewis concern.

By then his Rotting Hill flat was a derelict shell. Ruins had become his natural habitat. Every day had the imperatives of illness and aging.

"The failure of sight," he had written in his farewell to painting, "The Sea Mists of Winter" (1951), "will of course be worse from week to week until in the end I shall only be able to see the actual world through little patches in the midst of a blacked-out tissue."

Though he kept writing, his descent into the nameless had begun.

AGGRESSIVE VOLTAGE

Light, more light.
Goethe

"Pushed into an unlighted room, the door banged and locked for ever, I shall then have to light a lamp of aggressive voltage in my mind to keep at bay the night."

Lewis lit a flame in his mind.

But the winds of power routinely snuff out such egoism. Difference and dissent, tolerated in theory, pose a threat to those who want to shape opinion. And Lewis's independent flame—which he believed resembled a blow torch—was almost blown out.

Risking the powers allied against you: this is the code of awareness. Lewis demonstrated that freedom of speech is a matter of who manages the media, who controls access to the public. He dramatized throughout his cantankerous career that debate matters, and that if you talk truly to others as individuals, those who overhear will—however briefly—be powerless. He stated again that the worst crime for a citizen is to be unobservant, petty, asleep. He tested the limits of the intellectual's liberty in the post-war West.

Reading him is an act of mourning for what was called High Literacy. To read him is to remember what it means to read and write dangerously.

Now the problems he spotlighted are more insidious. The drama of the word plays to an emptying house. The solitary outlaw is both the writer and the reader. They are engaged in a strange exchange that is clandestine, even subversive, not in the best interest of an impulse-driven society suspicious of privacy.

Lewis's London flat, filled with paintings and books, like Pound's cage in Pisa or cell at St. Elizabeth's, may be exemplary images of the last literates: divided, dissenting, correcting the imbalances they perceive through opposition and creation, often losing the control and laughter they value, living long enough to see themselves self-condemned, in drafts and fragments, with doors banged and locked and eviction notices served, though still lighting aggressive voltage to hold back the night.

THE
QUIET
CIVIL WAR
OF
PIERRE
TRUDEAU

1

IN OUR TIME

The story of Pierre Elliott Trudeau is the story
of the man in the mask. That is why he came into
his own with TV. His image has been shaped by
the culture gap. Canada has never had
an identity. Instead, it has a cultural interface of
17th-century and 19th-century America.
Marshall McLuhan

For sixteen years a civil war was waged in Canada.
It was a war never publicly acknowledged because it was
never officially declared. There were few physical casu-
alties; nevertheless, the war was to the death. The death
was the genteel concept of the unilingual English state,
the peaceable kingdom, the country where nothing much
happened except nostalgia for a Loyalist past, a place without a vision of destiny, or the horrors of history. The civil
war had one champion, general, architect: Pierre Elliott
Trudeau. His goal: a bilingual cosmopolitan state unified
by a central-rationalist idea. His war was fought against

those who sought to fracture the nation into a loose federation; it was waged against the passive and dull, against isolationists ("the spirit of the age is divorce"). A refusal to recognize the agenda's imperative was branded treason. And Trudeau sometimes talked about treason. And intellectual combat. And a dream of reason. To win his war, Trudeau marshalled arsenals of stances and styles; he practised confrontational politics; taunted voters ("why should I sell your wheat?"); exhausted cabinet ministers; alienated those who had worked for the Liberal Party for decades; inspired coalitions and defections; seduced and bewildered commentators; married and then divorced the archetypal Flower Child; danced at discos; brought a constitution home; and, in an apparent paradox, launched an international peace crusade. And when he retired, and the Trudeau Party (once the Liberal Party) collapsed, inattentive pundits poked through the ruins asking, What happened? Under the leadership of Brian Mulroney, another Quebecker, the Progressive Conservatives—the only political party in the world with an inherent contradiction in their name—had won the largest parliamentary majority in Canadian history. The Trudeau era ended, as it had begun, in what seemed a surreptitiously staged *Götterdämmerung*. Trudeau entered self-imposed silence, a coda to a vocation of words. But along with Marshall McLuhan's perceptions on the impact of electronic circuitry ("we are living entirely by music") and Glenn Gould's ideas on the transmission of recorded sound, Trudeau's politics of reason had made time in Canada.

Time: 1968.

At age thirteen, I travelled with my parents to Ottawa to the Liberal convention to watch Trudeau, then the front runner in the leadership race.

It was the year of the assassin.

Martin Luther King was dead; Robert Kennedy would be murdered that summer; terrorists were in Quebec; Expo

'67 had ended in Montreal; Woodstock and Altamont were soon to be part of the decade's myths. For Canadians, Trudeau had appeared as if out of nowhere like an answer to the age's demand to be engaged. He would later prove to be a private/public anomaly, both frustrating and irritating; but for the moment he was the media's darling. That weekend at the Ottawa Civic Centre—hours spent among hot crowds—the party split into two extremes: the old right and the new left. The convention was a closer battle than people recall. Robert Winters, a businessman from Toronto (almost a prophetic prototype of Brian Mulroney), mounted an offensive against Trudeau on the fourth ballot. But Trudeau won, Winters came second, and a young cabinet minister named John Turner placed third. When Trudeau—slight, small, his Iroquois-like features set in a tight smile—stood up to wave, it was as if he were receiving a radical mandate.

Sixteen years later, I went back to Ottawa. The Race for the Rose was on; John Turner was the front runner in the campaign; Ronald Reagan was president of the United States; Fiscal Restraint and Overburdened Taxation were the issues; and McLuhan and Gould were dead. The public's mood: eager for relief.

A generation had grappled with questions of biography and history, with self-definition, while Trudeau was prime minister. "Finding a country....Inventing a country...." That was the slogan-like cry. For those of us born into the musicalized market, battling to recover our lost literacy and intellectual centre, Trudeau had often assumed the dimension of a historical force. He had demanded that we read our time, and he had been himself difficult to read.

Outside our borders, Canada and Trudeau had become synonymous. Inside, he was perceived as an alien storm. So I knew I had to go back to the Civic Centre on June 14, 1984.

A FAREWELL

*Adieux: Mettre des larmes dans sa voix
en parlant des Adieux de Fontainebleau.*
Flaubert

"See that fella there?" the elderly senator said. "Terrible fella. But...he's come back. It's astonishing! The party's reviving now that the beast is going!...Are you going to Nuremberg tonight? Let me tell you. Albert Speer wouldn't do it any better. Sieg Trudeau....Well, I can't be conned any more. Besides...no one calls me anyway. Not when I've grown so old and negative....Chrétien? Lord, no....He's one of *them*. I'm for Turner on Saturday."

"Oh, he's the best." A young woman delegate from Montreal was wistful. "We'll never see the likes of Trudeau again. The Number One PM....It's going to be hard to see him go. Turner? No way. I'm for Chrétien."

Fear and reverence, empathy and animosity. Emotional extremes were present early in the evening. Trudeau had centred attention absolutely upon himself. He had been the one-man army, a great man in a place that had not known notions of greatness. Reaction to him would be phrased in sullen or ecstatic absolutes. *La guerre* would not be quickly forgotten.

"He's a giant," a small businessman from Oakville said. "Unquestionably significant. Perhaps the most intelligent PM we've had. Nothing is the same after him. Even the other parties have had to recognize what Trudeau has accomplished with bilingualism and the social security net. These are lasting accomplishments."

"Thank God he's going. It'll be a return to normal. A return to...democracy." A man from Toronto shuddered. "No more complexity. No more condescension. A little peace and quiet at last, thank heavens. God. The mere mention of that man's name makes me shake.... You want to know why I hate him so much? No spontaneity.... Everything was calculated. Planned in advance. He had no sense of humour. You know [voice lowered to a confidential stage whisper] he was sexually neuter. Didn't do it at all!... Why am I here? Free tickets!"

Thus the audience was streaming in from the streets of Ottawa and the Exhibition Grounds (a cityscape of crumbling Victorian-style buildings; signs saying "Sheep and Swine" and "Home of the Ottawa Rough Riders").

WEAR A ROSE TONIGHT
IN HONOUR OF THE LEADER'S FAREWELL

At the Civic Centre—a cold bureaucratic pyramid with twentieth-century versions of flying buttresses—young girls in red smocks were handing out programs and buttons. The buttons were oblong, white on black, Trudeau in the middle, arms crossed, "enigmatic smile in place". (Reminder: use journalist's clichés when describing PET.) A red spot marked the rose in his lapel.

SHOW YOU WERE THERE

Red-covered books announced "Generation '84". On the back was a full-colour photograph of the Leader, legs apart, hands aggressively on his hips, staring off to the side. Location: the North. Message: explorers travel outside.

In Canada, Walden Pond is a glacier.

IN THE CURRENT

Here's a view of the world in which only music
has survived..."Synchronicity II" by the Police....
MTV announcer

The roaring began early.

In the evening, the sound was at first like a soft wave of murmuring, omnipresent and impossible to channel. The wave started to build, stepping up in pitch and volume, the rhythm in my ears, the sound enlarging and engulfing, amplified by halls and tunnels and stairwells and booths in the sports arena. Crowd sounds, the buzz from amplifiers, like an ocean of noise you became accustomed to while you looked for a seat, a place to stand, or wandered through packs of reporters. The wave summoned people as if in a huge swell. The centre of the magnetism: Trudeau. He embodied currency, and seduced, we were drawn. Delegates acted like tourists and bought roses, *Pierre* books, drawings, photographs, buttons, decals ("I'm a Liberal"), and posters. I saw election signs from 1968 that must have been specially preserved in plastic for just this occasion. And the roar continued to build until Trudeau arrived with his three sons and took his seat in the stands to the trumpet blast of the fight theme from *Rocky* and the show opened with rushes of whistling and clapping and hollering, "True-dough...True-dough... True-dough..."

Lights dim. Songs up. In the arena that resembled the inside of an enormous TV set, the wave peaked; and we were taken back in time.

The neon and plastic Canadian flag turned luminous and then dull, depending on which opera singer or pop star, politician or mimic, was paying tribute. Paul Anka sang, "And he did it...his way!" Trudeau smiled tightly. Down in what had become the press pit, the media people outnumbered the delegates and guests. Cameras (humming-clicking-buzzing) were positioned in batteries, on a raised platform, on banks of tripods, half aimed at Trudeau and his family, half aimed at the stage. The security was so lax that it would have been easy to walk up to the target, Trudeau, and fire a shot.

But the true star of this hymn to him was the documentary footage, the clips and stills edited together, and the sound track of voices. Scenes in black and white, and colour, showed Trudeau, younger and jauntier, teasing journalists and girls. Controversial moments like the War Measures Act were predictably muted. More images— of Trudeau meeting world leaders, presidents…fighting elections…strolling with his children. "True-dough…" the waves spoke.

And we were invited to sway to the rising and falling of memories and moods, each sequence drummed in with rock-'n'-roll breaks by Jimi Hendrix ("purple haze…is in my brain…"), the Police ("every step you take…I will be watching you…"), and the Rolling Stones ("hey, the storm is threatening…my very life today…")—an electronic tide churned up as a prelude to the words of one of the more literate politicians in the western world. "At the centre of the technological debate is a new kind of listener," Glenn Gould wrote in 1966, "a listener more participant in the musical experience. The emergence of this mid-twentieth century phenomenon is the greatest achievement of the record industry." For this new kind of listener, the show's organizers knew that ideas would be secondary to the acoustic wave.

Trudeau remained unmoved throughout the musical maelstrom. He seemed absorbed by a self-contained meditation. What was on his mind? These were surely not the songs he listened to at home. Perhaps he reflected on the mythic allusions and ruthless actions he had taken to divide and dominate the Canadian political arena. He of course had access to the hidden stories behind the rock-show theatrics.

1968: I had observed Trudeau sitting aloof in the midst of politicians, friends, and alluring mini-skirted women from Montreal. They were waiting for the fourth-ballot results. Like a still point in the turning whirl, Trudeau had radiated a similar serenity then. When he became prime minister, his cool would provoke both the respect and the frenzy of onlookers. On that Thursday night in 1984 he was again the solitary in public, asking us to complete his picture.

Then I knew why I had come.

The event could have been watched on television. But Trudeau was a political chameleon, the elusive stranger who had never quite been one of us. Civil wars are fought between brothers. The audience at the Civic Centre revealed the rifts: Trudeau had become a focus of wild fantasies and fears. How could this polarized perception have occurred?

Trudeau had written *Federalism and the French Canadians*; he was a thinker familiar with languages and ideas. His accomplishments: the Official Languages Act (1969) and the Constitution Act (1982). This concentration on the word made Trudeau different; for anyone who is literate today is eccentric. ("Intellectuals always find Trudeau interesting," a Liberal Party worker muttered sourly to me.)

In office, that private intellectual had expanded into unsettling omnipresence through TV, radio, and newspapers. For sixteen years we had played and replayed him, dismembering, remembering, amused and bemused. When the electronic media creates gods, politics becomes metaphysics. So we struggled to identify him, giving him tags and titles, from dictator to devil, from angel to magus. He seemed to move mysteriously on frontiers we couldn't apprehend. Strange questions: was he something recreated? Was the quiet civil war fought with us, with the political system, or with himself? Who was that person receiving the icons and songs, at a convention held, with devious planning, in Orwell's 1984?

Tear a man from the web of illusion and delusion. Present him cold, clear. If it is possible.

Canada had accelerated from colonialism to modernism in two decades. This man with the hybrid Anglophone-Francophone name of Pierre Elliott Trudeau was a manifestation of that abrupt transition. Names have everything to do with the nebulous world of identity that convulses intellectuals. Suddenly while I stood on the convention floor, close to someone I had been fascinated by for years, I understood that you couldn't escape from the obsession with the nameless and the unnameable: you had to engage your milieu and the figures in it.

Music off. The arena seemed to breathe in. Murmuring; rustling; a soft hiss from air conditioners. Police assembled into position: like walls, they cordoned off a route up to the stage. And Trudeau walked up to deliver a speech without notes or a teleprompter. A near-silence as if in suspense. The arena-turned-TV underwent a second transformation. It was alive with watching.

2

PUBLIC FACE

...the ability to do what is appropriate is a matter of
trained skill and of talent, the knowledge of
what is appropriate to a particular occasion is a
matter of practical sagacity.
Cicero

Trudeau began in French with Rimbaud's "Ma
Bohème" and spoke of dreams. Then he shifted into English.

*And when I saw those, heard those, tributes, and saw
those film clips, I wanted to tell you basically two
things. First, how pleased I was, how grateful I was,
that my three boys were able to see that the line of
business that their dad was in...had some importance
for this country. And they will know that the time I
spent away from them was working with Canadians, but
particularly—they were very nice Canadians who are in
the Liberal Party. I thought that these fifteen past years*

*in a certain sense were the period of adolescence of
our country, the coming of age....*

After sixteen years, Pierre Elliott Trudeau had changed
little in his physical appearance. He was paunchier, grey-
ing; his face was creased, tight around the cheek bones,
baggy under the eyes. "He's had a facelift," a photographer whispered half-admiringly beside me. Yet Trudeau, a
small person, emanated size. It is true that small actors—
Dustin Hoffman is one—can emanate presence by a force
of personal projection, as if they are taking on a whole
group at once through the camera lens. An experiment
performed later with videotaped images of Trudeau at the
convention showed that at fast forward he remained still;
at fast forward he looked the same. Everyone else in the
frame became frantic. And there on stage he was again
still, limiting his gestures to hand slashes, punches of air,
tilts of the head, and the occasional well-timed grimace.

*And I won't fall into the trap of talking about those
fifteen-sixteen years together. You delegates, you Liberals,
are here in this city* [The accusatory second-person "you"
reminded us that Trudeau could attack at any moment. Attack, however, did not seem to be on his mind.] *to choose
the person who will lead our party into the future. But
it seems to me that as I saw those various events rushing before our eyes...I discovered something we always
knew...*

He sounded bland; but that was what was required.
From Trudeaumania to his one defeat in 1979, he had
ranged across Canada, receiving insults, kisses, jeers. He
had travelled. He could now provide the proper tone and
point of view for a crowd eager for the pleasures of Big
Media. He had learned that if you speak without notes,
you engage the audience's attention. Trudeau was never
as effective when he read from a prepared text.

A country is something that is built out of certain basic values. "Get on with it," a photographer grumbled. *Those values that for instance we see in the Canadian Charter of Rights, which for the first time gives all of us an identity rooted in a constitution....*

"Yeah," another cameraman said, "and the way you stayed in power was by the goddamned fags and Jews." *We have the inheritance of Locke and Jefferson and Montesquieu and Acton and Mill. And they taught us that problems that men create can be solved by men of goodwill...if they apply reason to those problems. And that is what Liberals do. They see the difficulties. They look for rational solutions. They make sure that reason prevails over prejudice....*

Trudeau positioned himself and his government. The list of authors and politicians was not name-dropping— though he could intimidate others through allusions to intellectuals he knew most hadn't read. An intelligible line developed, Jefferson to Mill. Tonight Trudeau was the teacher who spoke out to individuals—if he could find any. The emerging line: liberty and rationality, reason prevailing over prejudice. He recited definitions of activist politics within the democratic system; Trudeau had never advocated the overthrow of the whole political-social structure.

Liberals...confront the powerful. They confound the secure. They challenge the conventional. They're asking questions all the time. They're looking for answers to those problems which prevent a country from fulfilling its destiny....

Probing...pushing...the need to affront complacency and convention...agitation, irritation—these bring involvement. Trudeau could have been describing the role of the individual in rebellion. Yet these were prescriptions for social action.

And there was his recurrent word destiny. From "destine", to ordain, appoint, doom; the Latin, "destina", means "a support" and links with "stand", as in "taking a stand", and with "destination". Destiny was not fatalism: free movement established contours of meaning. What was the destination? Canada redefined from the days of St. Laurent, Diefenbaker, and Pearson.

Trudeau began a partisan recitation of the accomplishments of the Liberal Party; he recalled 1877 and Wilfrid Laurier. He modulated back into French for that portion. Again speech patterns were altered; we heard accented rhythms and stronger intonations. *And Mackenzie King after him...who saw that the weak in our society needed protection...*Trudeau had leaped from French into English with the uttering of King's name. Mixing modes is mixing moods. It was a way of changing his relationship with segments of the audience; though he was aware that many wouldn't understand the French. The history lesson gained speed. Lester Pearson was cited. And the capping hyperbole: *These are leaders.*

Then came Trudeau's only stumble. *Liberalism is not only a party of purses—purposes...*A recovery; but "purses" lingered with me. All parties, political or otherwise, are parties of purses: lobby groups who exact their own "interest rates". Trudeau, a wealthy man ("Just a rich kid playing politics" was an often-heard remark), knew about money power. He was True-dough: the real cash. But the presence of money power was not his subject; we would have to explore that presence later in the convention and during the election in September when the two major parties ran corporation men.

Trudeau's voice rebounded off the tractable crowd; he did not shout (to whisper is enough when you are amplified), until he came to the constitution: *Fifty-four years of frustration...and we said to the people...do you want a constitution of your own?* His remarkably simple rhetorical technique of lists, summaries, chronologies, and questions kept his audience on edge, waiting for the polemical punch.

One thing was odd. For someone who used poetry as much as Trudeau did, his own speech lacked imagery and metaphor. He emphasized argument and feared emotional extremes. Beyond reason, he was conscious of the consequences of irrational force.

Trudeau's cardinal concern was to join thinking with feeling; he distrusted mindless emotion. *"Ratio et oratio"*: reason and speech. Ratio is balance or *ratio*-nality: the balancing of the senses that is common sense. Trudeau at his noblest stood for balance, rationality, and a reaching out to the common sense of others.

Remember fifteen years ago our territorial sea was a piddling three miles. And now two hundred miles...a territorial zone...

If there was one rhetorical figure Trudeau favoured, it was antithesis. He used dialectical opposites to exaggerate the other's position and then slid in a synthesis that sounded eminently reasonable.

*So remember this, because tonight I'm stepping down as your leader...and in two days we will be choosing a new leader and you will find me there with you following him...because we have much to do...*Trudeau spoke as if his accomplishments were self-evident. He had set the co-ordinates for how he wanted his record to read: liberal tradition and conventions. Scholars could now follow up on the precedents of Locke and Mill. But I suspected that Trudeau wasn't finished.

In the stands, there was a low rumble of grumblings, mumblings, and uncomfortable stretchings. Post-literacy made us all jittery, attracted to misty emotion, mass exhibitionism. We had the nervous urge to switch to a commercial.

Trudeau did not oblige the restless. He was offering a politics of ideas. Around me, cameramen were vying for angles; reporters listened to headsets for instructions and murmured into microphones: "What?...yeah …yeah…yeah…."

And Trudeau had time to quote Rimbaud over the gathering heaves of impatience. Then: *We will dream some more. Our hopes are high, our faith in the people is great, our courage is strong, and our dreams for this beautiful country will never…*[voice lingering; softly] *die….*

Dreams! he said again. Applause. He opened his arms to the stands. *Les enfants de la patrie* [two beats]. *Come on kids.*

It was almost impossible to resist the picture of Trudeau surrounded by his three sons. Even at that instant he was brazenly aware of the impact of public metaphor. And the wave rolled over us again, "True-dough…."

Dreams. He had spoken of the need to see beyond the temporary, the troubled, and the tainted. It was a clichéd appeal. Yet in our fantasyland of spotlights like lasers, rock-'n'-roll nights, the neon sex of Las Vegas, there were consumers who lived in dreamlands of fast foods, the shining, and the sensations of speed and pornography. That was clearly not the dream Trudeau addressed.

Trudeau was a pragmatic idealist, a tough adversary, a man acquainted with the muck of political power grubbing. So when he spoke of dreams, I was, for a moment, not the skeptic. It was as if he recalled an ideal of enrichment and enlightenment, a dream after reality's slam, the dream of a just society where tension, paradox, difference, and contradiction would suspend the invasion of ignorance and night; it was a hope worthy of attention because it resulted not from sightless flight but from the shock of entanglement, crisis, and complexity. Trudeau saw the potential of history happening here. He had perceived that junctures of choice teach freedom, and that liberty is earned through vigilance, debate, and action. He summoned memories of Martin Luther King's "I have a dream" speech uttered before Trudeau himself was elected prime minister; he recalled Kennedy's "The dream never dies" speech; and he gave his words the tone of a place as yet untested, untouched. Something happened. Above the snide comments, the boredom, and the bitter memories (everyone remembered a Trudeau flip-flop), Canada was, for this man, "a beautiful place". That was why we had listened to him in 1968, and it was why so many, in the press especially, acted like jilted over-eroticized lovers later. Paradoxically, Trudeau's message was not just for politics but for the reflective mind.

On stage, he gave the crowd an encore: a pirouette between security guards. Eees and aaahs: a flurry of clapping and cheers. Then he was gone. Lights up. Music off.

The skeptic stepped back. I was to find over the next two days that it would be phantoms we'd be chasing, not Trudeau's dream of reason. Reminder: a strain divided the peaceable kingdom. Most were delighted to see "the awful...impolite man" retire ("he undermined the democratic system"). And there was more.

A crucial question: how do you convey mind (content) in a medium devoted to icon, formula, and sell-schlock (the con)? Behind the inflation and deflation, there was another ominous question. The electric media are synonymous with politics today; and yet those media are the largest creator of mass sensibility since the British invented the concentration camp in the Boer War. Individual perspective is erased by the TV and radio blitz of cliché. Now political campaigns live on reaction. Irrationality rules.

To recover the creature (Walker Percy's fine phrase), you had to single out an individual from reproduction and noise, hypnotic entertainment and the persuasion of masks. You had to restore the creature to singularity and paradox.

There was a way to tip the ratio back: Trudeau's writings.

INTELLECTUAL TERRORISM

The two-party system of modern parliaments uses the
psychological structure of opposing armies.
In England in the Civil War these actually existed,
although unwillingly. No one likes killing
his own countrymen....But the two factions remain;
they fight on, but in a form of warfare which
has renounced killing.
Elias Canetti

The subplot of Trudeau's speech was written more than twenty years before and published as *Le Fédéralisme et la société canadienne-française* and in English in 1968 under the title *Federalism and the French Canadians*. A rereading reveals the clarity of Trudeau's thoughts on language, nationalism, and the necessity of debate. A literate politician in the nineteenth century was expected (recall Disraeli); in the late twentieth, he may be an anomaly. A politician's literacy will not guarantee that he or she will be a superior manager of government policy. Yet treat Trudeau like a writer: perceive his mind shaped by words. Focus on this one book in translation. Then the essays become his blueprint for navigating in power, a declaration of war on English Canada's insidious passivity, a test of the limits of the status quo.

First paragraph

The only constant factor to be found in my thinking over the years has been opposition to accepted opinions. Had I applied this principle to the stock market, I might have made a fortune. I chose to apply it to politics, and it led me to power—a result I had not really desired, or even expected.

Second paragraph

In high school, when the only politics I was taught was history, I had already made up my mind to swim against the tide. But what was then an ill-defined reflex against intellectual regimentation became a conscious choice as soon as I went to university.

Phrases follow like: "society in Quebec fell under the domination of the Union Nationale....I fought this regime...."; "I remained a fierce supporter"; "and so, to defend federalism, I entered politics in 1965"; "the federal Liberal party, which I had so often condemned while it was at the height of its power...."

Like the man, the language bristles. Style is character. Here the tone is vigorous, the rhythms emphatic, the diction assured. We sense presence; the writing exudes power. It is self-centred: the authority can make the author. Trudeau uses himself as an organizing principle, a common device in essays and journalism; it shouldn't surprise us. But the kind of self-centred style we find is not the narcissistic-nobody style that we find in talk-show celebrity autobiographies or in the subterfuge of political memoirs ("I don't remember Watergate...."). The "I" evokes individuality. "Our I is our vocation," Ortega y Gasset writes. The first page of a collection taken from *Cité Libre* and other lectures and sources sets out a tone that will persist through various reshapings.

"Swim against the tide"; "opposition to accepted opinion...." The role Trudeau assumes is clear: the guerrilla politician. The voice is in startling contrast to the elegiac style he used at his farewell. Yet that first paragraph, which seems to make a virtue of inconsistency (Emerson: "A foolish consistency is the hobgoblin of little minds"), establishes the stance that Trudeau would consistently hold.

He is not praising inconsistency of course. It is tension. A static social scene will have as its effect a static, repressive art: the paintings of Alex Colville, the theories of Northrop Frye. Discontinuity—or discord—invites association. From the first paragraph we understand that Trudeau's idea of participatory democracy has nothing to do with consensus: it is centred in challenge, contention, engagement—intellectual terrorism.

"Opposition..."; "reflex against..."; "I fought...". The force of this prose is channelled by self-discipline. The style is clear, that clarity earned through self-criticism. An analytical ability is a talent to conscientiously resee. He revises to be.

The book shows that Trudeau accepted the framework of the liberal democratic process, the tradition of reformation and criticism. When the War Measures Act was implemented, there were shouts that Trudeau was a dictator, a militarist, despite his reputation as a radical. But Trudeau's polemics indicated structures he would always work within: friction between established order (humanist tradition) and innovative energy. In the forum of intellectual exchange, ideas could be as deadly as letter bombs. Reform came from an acceptance of rational ground. "I do not think that using dynamite in a country that enjoys freedom of speech can be considered a sign of rational progress." *Caveat lector.* Mental dynamite does the job; sparks come from the turbulent spirit: enlightenment results from turning verbal fire toward advocacy of "the greatest good". "I early realized that ideological systems are the true enemies of freedom," Trudeau says. And: "Men do not exist for states," he writes in "Quebec and the Constitutional Problem"; "states are created to make it easier for men to attain some of their common objectives." He would not try to give rigid theoretical consistency to his thinking. That would lead to the logical result of dialectics: totalitarianism. The end process: the Gulag, home for those who cannot fit in with systematic planning.

He recognizes a form of totalitarianism in the liberal democracy: "the tyranny of public opinion....For public opinion seeks to impose its domination over everything." Another "instrument of oppression": the mass media. "They follow their customers and are therefore always lagging behind reality."

Trudeau concludes

> In any case, I never claimed to speak "on behalf" of anyone; if the Party does not agree with my opinions, it can repudiate me; if my constituents do not, they can elect someone else....To "ready-made" or second-hand ideas, I have always preferred my own. They form the substance of this book....

Here he asserts his independence and his desire to subject himself to peril. These characteristics of the solitary would later enrage us in our placid backwater of history, and would have a devastating consequence for the Liberal Party after Trudeau resigned.

"Halfway between sermon and story," William H. Gass says, "the essay interests itself in the narration of ideas—in the unfolding—and the conflict between philosophies or other points of view becomes a drama in its hand; systems are seen as plots and concepts as character." The essay has personified the inquiring spirit from Montaigne and Emerson to Gore Vidal and Norman

Mailer. So it is a shock to realize when reading *Federalism and the French Canadians* that Trudeau is a political-social thinker who writes a more vigorous prose than the general literati. Good prose comes from good conversation. And there is provocative talk in these essays. The reader then experiences the delight intellectuals felt on their initial contact with Trudeau's work. An individual with a mind to back up his arguments, he could be a demanding opponent.

A review by Barry Callaghan in 1968, then literary editor of *The Telegram*, appraises Trudeau's "pragmatic vision" of Canada as a "brilliant prototype for a truly pluralistic and polyethnic society". Callaghan concludes with a prescient insight into the dichotomies that drove Trudeau.

> ...there is a curious streak to Trudeau, a streak that is an integral part of his strength, and I suspect that M. Trudeau's unique understanding of the authoritarian nature of his country [sic] stems from *the tensions that exist within himself.*...It seems that Pierre Elliott Trudeau is determined to prove that there is nothing merely emotional about himself, nor about the people of Canada, if only they will learn to have an honest opinion of themselves. (My emphasis)

In this review, Trudeau is described as a Jansenist; it will not be the last time he is so categorized."...the tensions that exist within himself"; "determined to prove that there is nothing merely emotional about himself...". But Callaghan's dualism and the theological label are too schematic. Contraries are convenient intellectual fictions: they cannot define the whole person. And what Callaghan does not say is that the entire individual must be immersed, as if he is drowning, before he can swim against the current.

Nevertheless, who else saw the fury about to be un-leashed? Or that Trudeau would balance splits within himself that were realizations of national collisions? Trudeau's desire to alter the style and structure of Canadian society was the core of his agenda. From "A Constitutional Declaration of Rights"

A constitutional change recognizing broader rights with respect to the two official languages would add a new dimension to Confederation.

We are not going to be caught in a posture of immobility.

Again, Trudeau's voice—pushed forward by questions (probes), and with italicized words for oral emphasis—demands that Quebec not be isolated in Confederation, that intellectuals take an aggressive role in Canada. He detested the brand of nationalism that separated people. His nationalism had none of the shrill polarizations that were popular in central Canada in the 1960s. "The whole Canadian system of government," he writes in "The Practice and Theory of Federalism", "would be improved by creative tensions between the central, the provincial, and even the municipal administrations."

While *Federalism and the French Canadians* is not a masterpiece of political writing, it does show that Trudeau would have had a vital role as a social critic.

However, the unresolved tension in his prose style is his own recognized emotion/reason dualism. His style suggests an encounter with someone imposing checks and balances on himself. Emotions seethe under the sentences. Contempt and sarcasm mingle. The essays also lack sensuality; he avoids poetic imagery, word plays, what Ezra Pound calls melopoeia, the music of words. Public metaphor would do: canoeing in the north, for example.

Trudeau's fear of the irrational is subtle. It is not emotion *per se* he eschews. It is the mindless emotion of mass impulse. Each person has to be appealed to individually. Nationalism was for him a tribal instinct. Quebec politics *en masse* threatened to become herd politics: extremist, mystical, narcissistic. Tribal politics were anti-democratic, and the media played into that tribalism. Yet he understood this power and was willing to use it. That is why the Jansenist tag is inadequate. Jansenism is a fringe wing of Catholic theology that severs the world into a Manichean split of good versus evil: good is located in the mind, evil in the body. Trudeau was afraid of feeling propelled by sentimental violence, of a condition in which reason and intelligence would not have a role. He saw Canadian society on the edge between two extremes: entrenched culture in English Canada, warfare in Quebec.

> This is what I call *la nouvelle trahison des clercs*: this self-deluding passion of a large segment of our thinking population for throwing themselves headlong— intellectually and spiritually—into purely escapist pursuits.

> The upper levels of our society suffer from paralysing inertia.

> Nationalism, as an emotional stimulus directed at an entire community, can indeed let loose unforeseen powers. History is full of this, called variously chauvinism, racism, jingoism, and all manner of crusades, where right reasoning and thought are reduced to rudimentary proportions.

> I am not in a frantic hurry to change the constitution, simply because I am in a frantic hurry to *change reality*. (My emphasis)

Altered states! The dream of revolutionary thinkers (the Marxist: "You do not have to understand reality in order to change it.") and artists (Rimbaud: "*Le poète se fait* voyant *par un long, immense et raisonné* dérèglement *de tous les sens.*").

We have seen the effects of endless revolution and experimentation. Arrest kills the spirit; immobility is paralysis. But innovation for its own sake ends, if it can be said to end, in the exaltation of the ephemeral. The consumer is the product of revolutionary zeal: insatiable, he has to be constantly fed. In the laboratory world of William Burroughs's *Naked Lunch*, he is the junkie terrorist, jaded in his sensibilities and tastes, demanding to be shown things he has never seen. Speed kills. Yet immobility leads to another kind of death. The result: the voyeur. The struggle therefore is to balance a desire for enlightenment, which is progressive, and a recognition of the limits of the vulnerable person. Trudeau, however, was a politician who accepted certain structures in society and who recognized that mobility of mind depended on friction within that tradition. Thus the strains: internal/external, emotion/reason, passivity/commitment. Trudeau's dualisms did involve a shocking threat to security. Rebels attack individual targets, the specifics of an abuse; revolutionaries seek to undermine the whole. And Pierre Elliott Trudeau would henceforth be an eighteenth-century man of intellect and action balancing the twin extremes of dreaming and terrorism, his career like an object lesson of what happens when reform values and the spirit of Voltaire clash with electromagnetism.

Trudeau's other important work is *Les Cheminements de la politique*. The remaining texts and essays in English have interest only to historians. *Two Innocents in Red*

China (1968), co-written with Jacques Hébert, is a memoir of a journey to the Far East. The title is meant to echo Mark Twain's *Innocents Abroad* . "The citizens of our democracy should know more about China." Dull diary jottings abound. "Wednesday, 14 September....London is a good town and Alec Guinness is a wonderful actor....Thursday, 15 September....A meeting in Trudeau's room to decide whether we will go to Brecht's *The Life of Galileo*." There are two moments of half wit: Trudeau is referred to, deadpan, as "The Leader"; and "Monday, 17 October....Chinese Marxists are like Quebec theologians. On questions of religion and sex, they lose their sang-froid." (An in-joke for the Quebec circle.) Trudeau's literary output, apart from interviews and some prefaces and introductions, has been slight.

He no doubt had other things on his mind while he was prime minister.

Trudeau has announced that he will not write his memoirs. This is unfortunate since he is one of the few contemporary Canadian politicians whose memoirs would have genuine relevance. (Disraeli: "I'd rather write a good book than read one.") Whatever happens, *Federalism and the French Canadians* remains the indispensable manifesto. For as those at the Farewell either complained or explained, nothing was the same afterwards.

When I reread Trudeau's book, I sense the authentic stress in his language. It is like encountering the rhythms of one locked into a battle that could only be resolved by confronting what was within himself and the national psyche. The effect: of a mind thinking, not a unified theory. This writer who scorned isolationists, emotional extremism, and the intellectuals' Trivial Pursuit (a Canadian invention) was ready to implement his dream of reason.

Against paralysis, he would pose stress, effort, and the ability to play (flip a position). He had values, but he was prepared to be unprincipled.

Journalist: "How far will you go?"
Trudeau: "Just watch me."

The exchange took place on Parliament's steps after the War Measures Act, a bill enacted against guerrillas who used real weapons.

DISSENT INTO RULE

*Machiavélisme: Mot violent et terrible qu'on ne
doit prononcer qu'en frissonnant.
Machiavel: Haine contre ne pas l'avoir lu.*
Flaubert

Controversy is the spirit of the active life: how to argue and to criticize; reason against reason in the complexity of contrast. But a controversialist depends on being an opposition force. What happens when an intellectual joins the mainstream and runs for government?

Trudeau was a product of the Quiet Revolution in Quebec, a war fought to free the political system from the shackles of clerical domination and the inward-turned nationalism of the Québécois intelligentsia. He went to Ottawa with an agenda: give Quebec a stronger part to play in Confederation, enshrine bilingualism (minority rights), and defeat a nationalism that sought to isolate French Canada "in a corner of North America". When Trudeau became prime minister, he detonated a quiet civil war with the rest of Canada.

Trudeau was a born outsider. The cadences of his prose show how difficult it would be to impose anything on such a person. All direction had to be generated from within. His background encouraged him: strong mother, absent father, wealthy family, private-school education,

Jesuit training. A traveller, man of the world; hence hostile to the nets of time and institutions. He could have stayed a professional dilettante, but he didn't. He plunged inside. Shake up your world and you shake up yourself. Government is run by insiders. Ottawa, a city of gossip, is itself a place of insiders. How do you fit into that clubhouse? You can't; so you start your own. And Trudeau built a massive one: he centralized authority in the PMO; he created theoretical structures; he was compelled to be a bureaucrat, and organization quickly became a thing for itself. Green papers, white papers, committees, task forces, enlarged departments, regional desks, technocrats, inner circles, memos, theories: the intellectual became politician. Departments appeared like swollen autonomous units with mandates for independent programs. The spreading system looked faceless. A hard irony here. One of the most individual PMs this country has produced created a system that seemed at odds with any individuality. Yet he stood at the centre while government was perceived to swell like an infectious disease. In government by exploration, limits could be found through reaction. And soon there was reaction. The centre stood clear; but the margins were fuzzy. And the hatred for Trudeau grew.

Out of the fighter's stance, away from the voice we find in *Federalism and the French Canadians,* Trudeau's guerrilla politics couldn't work in the collegial system he cultivated in Privy Council committees. "He was never autocratic," it is reported in George Radwanski's *Trudeau* (1978); "it all got bogged down in talk," Richard Gwyn repeats in *The Northern Magus* (1980).

When the explorer who fights the current joins the current, he is no longer an effective navigator; he is just drifting with the rest. And the Trudeau government in the 1970s was often lost in drift and doldrums.

There is a process at work in the lives of those who are touched by a desire for greatness. You begin by attacking the energies you disagree with; yet at some point you end up embodying those forces. Balances swing. In power, you become what you formerly assaulted; and from that moment on, you are a target.

Example: Trudeau's French, even in translation, is taut; his Jacobin-like fervour blazes from every exclamation point. After sixteen years as prime minister, his healthy aggression was homogenized into bureaucratic babyfood (by others?). Consider this from the Souvenir Edition of the book handed out free at the convention (later offered for sale at bookstores).

> We have come a long way together, met challenges, worked side by side for those ideals we deemed to be both liberal and Liberal. In the process, we have contributed mightily to that unique experiment in nation building that we know as Canada.
>
> I leave the Party's leadership and the office of the Prime Minister in my belief that both the country and the Party remain strong and vigorous.
>
> For my part, the journey has been a most happy one and I thank you for making it possible.

The French on the opposite page is livelier. Did Trudeau actually do the writing himself? The prose has turned flat and forgettable. (Trudeau's prefaces for coffee-table books have the same deadened style.)

It is tempting to say that he allowed the bureaucracy to bury his individuality. But perhaps there are deeper reasons. Did he allow others to write these harmless squibs in order to maintain control? Blandness might have appealed to Canadians. Was Trudeau more comfortable writing in French than in English? More conscious of the effect his sarcasm would have in Quebec? A review of the English portion of his speech at the Civic Centre shows a reliance on the "and" connective to sustain his recital of accomplishments. Biblical overtones aside, Trudeau is not only a trained speaker, but he is also a natural one who knows how to get his effects. That night he used a verbal pillow to soften his farewell. In Ottawa, Trudeau's polemics became relaxed: or is it that he felt he couldn't depend on an intellectually vigorous response? It may be that many could not tolerate the unrest he could unlock with language. Interesting: almost every "fuck off" or middle-finger salute he gave was aimed at English Canadians, rarely at French.

Second example: the fierce anti-nationalist who had likened such movements to National Socialism (Hitlerism) became a reluctant nationalist himself. On this issue Trudeau did listen to his advisers. Yet the identity issue plunged to the roots of our uneasiness. "Who are we?": the banner of the mid-century. So the great pronoun debate ensued: "I", "you", "he", "she", even "it". The so-called liberation movements revolved around identifying a private self. Trudeau's quiet civil war then broke out in other directions: "you" against the established "I".

Scanned with the eye of publicity, Trudeau was different from anything we had experienced. He was given a romantic mask, "the Northern Magus". A popular joke said, "Did you hear about Trudeau's accident on the lake?" "No, what happened?" "A motorboat ran into him while he was taking a walk." He was the chilly "Pro-consul"; "Imperial Trudeau"; the Philosopher King; "that Jew"; sexually ambivalent, possibly bisexual (another duality). Trudeau soon understood the secret of staying in power: mystery. Never disclose your full intentions; pull strings without appearing to do so. The age of anxiety has passed;

high speeds and paranoia dictate the social mood. And so Trudeau threw out tidbits to distract people: he danced with starlets; he appeared at a football game wearing a Bohemian cape, like a dandy aesthete; he fired off snappy put-downs, and fired elastic bands at reporters; he gave the despised press a show. (They would like that; they would be thrown off the scent.) While he played the fool in public, behind the scenes he could pursue his agenda of change: a bilingual, republican Canada. Trudeau said during some lunging scrum, "If you move quickly enough, no one can define you." So he threw out questions—Where do you stand? What do you believe?—in intellectual combat with his audience, as if he were more satirist than politician. "I'd like to kill the prick," reporters grumbled. And the rage continued to rise like a hurricane of hate.

Was he a "Sartrean Existential I"? or a Romantic? These were ways of appearing before a mass public that would not tolerate a naked person. Wyndham Lewis said

> Romance is what partakes of the marvellous, the extreme, the unusual. Advertisement is the apotheosis of the marvellous and the unusual....The spirit of advertisement and boost lives and has its feverish being in a world of hyperbolic suggestion; it is also the trance or dream world of the hypnotist....(*Time and Western Man*)

We are all Romantics today, given the hallucinative-heightening powers at work in the social-cultural arena. Trudeau recognized this; it doesn't matter whether his was an intuitive or intellectual discovery. However, he was not romantic in temperament: he was analytical, linear; he accepted society as the field of action; he thought about architectonics, the long-range plan. Like Glenn Gould, a classicist comfortable with Bach and sculpted shapes, Trudeau had an eighteenth-century predilection for clarity,

self-discipline, and privacy that collided with the stereotyping devices of electric technology. The poets he quoted
tended to be the Romantics; but the poet he quoted on
memorable occasions was that wiliest and most ambivalent modern, Robert Frost.

It was television that made Trudeau a creature of
magical survival capabilities. Not surprisingly, Marshall
McLuhan offered advice to Trudeau over the years through
an extensive correspondence and personal discussion.
McLuhan had devoted an admiring review in the *New York
Review of Books* in 1968 to *Federalism and the French
Canadians*.

(McLuhan's review was, ironically, reprinted in 1970
in *Canada: A Guide to the Peaceable Kingdom.* The
edition contains an essay by Richard Kostelanetz on Glenn
Gould: "...Gould takes the cue of Marshall McLuhan, a
local acquaintance, and makes the telephone an extension
of himself.")

A study needs to be written on the influence that
McLuhan has had on North American politics. What is not
understood is the impact McLuhan's ideas had on another
figure from the 1960s, Richard Nixon. Joe McGinniss's
The Selling of the President describes the repackaging of a
candidate for television; Norman Mailer's *Miami and the
Siege of Chicago* records the rebirth of a politician whose
career had, seemingly, been terminated by the Kennedys.

An anecdote survives that describes McLuhan's talent
to persuade. At the Centre for Culture and Technology,
McLuhan lounged in his armchair, thick cigar burning in
his fingers, and waved a letter he had written to Trudeau.
He explained: after the Liberal defeat of 1979, a spent
Trudeau retreated to the north for a canoeing trip; when
he returned to opposition leader duties, he was sporting a
freshly grown grey beard. "If you want to stay in politics,"
McLuhan said, "shave off the beard...you look retired."
A few weeks later, the beard was gone. Soon Trudeau's

return to politics would be cunningly stage-managed, and he would begin his most active period of political engagement.

February 1980: Trudeau ran against Tory leader Joe Clark—whose name telegraphed Joke Lark and hence eventual defeat by unforgiving voters. Trudeau won a majority government and a mandate to retrieve a constitution.

there is no escape from politics, nor should there be....

the day of language barriers is finished....

My political action, or my theory...insomuch as I can be said to have one—can be expressed very simply: create counterweights. (*Federalism and the French Canadians*)

At the 1980–82 constitutional conferences following the Quebec referendum, we at last saw *la guerre civile* fully dramatized. Trudeau undermined the premiers' concentration by staring deadpan at the ceiling, shutting his eyes and appearing to doze, gazing down at his lap, scrutinizing foes, and reading back another's remarks in a slightly mocking tone that reduced his opponent to sputtering outrage. He won situations with what TV commentators called unfair tactics. The dilemma: most did not understand Trudeau's agenda. They had not read his book, the manifesto that revealed the hard contour of his aim.

The Plain Citizen who can read the ground of a debate or an issue has the liberty to make intelligent discriminations. For those who do not themselves have political power, understanding the rhetoric of an event is what Wyndham Lewis meant by the art of being ruled. It is the art of being attentive to what is off camera as well as on camera. Elias Canetti's *Crowds and Power* also provides points for twentieth-century piloting: his concern is for the reader or receiver who must pilot in lightning spectacles. When the effects of power become invisible because of electric speed, then the Plain Citizen must make them visible through his or her own vivid charting.

The Constitutional Conference resulted in patriation, the Charter of Rights, and more power for the Supreme Court. Trudeau's demand for strong centralized government ("Who will speak for Canada?") was based on his ideal of intelligible line (federal government) and decentralized margins (provincial autonomy). His federalism was a mosaic. Lawyer, writer, wealthy man, politician: he had spent decades preparing for the moment when he could act.

Typically, the provincial premiers, with a few exceptions, reacted as if they had been punched. The final irony: Quebec refused to sign the accord.

Trudeau was not obviously disturbed. ("...I never claimed to speak 'on behalf' of anyone." *Federalism and the French Canadians*.) He knew that separatism had been defeated for his lifetime.

Hazard an analogy. Not to a Canadian statesman of the past. Trudeau had few peers and, other than Wilfrid Laurier and John A. Macdonald, few predecessors. Perhaps we should compare him with those authoritative dreamers who re-established their nations on alternative courses: Cromwell, Lincoln, and Garibaldi. Trudeau's quiet civil war ended in bitterness, resentment, and his own megalomania; but that is the pattern.

Here was a very complex man who never, with all
his dazzling renown, managed to satisfy himself....He
never believed that he knew the answers to everything;
it was, rather, that when he made up his mind to a
thing, the fact that he had done so made him right. What
he prided himself upon above all was the instinct that
enabled him, he believed, to sense the movement of
history so that he could profit by a process of which
others were oblivious...He created and propagated his
own legend, of course; but it takes two to make a
legend...

This is Edward Crankshaw on the creator of modern
Germany, Otto von Bismarck. Not to strain the analogy
too far, Trudeau waged his campaigns peacefully, in the
tradition of Canadian society. Exception: the War Measures Act. Yet he understood the existential fact of his
location: the fact of size and place. The ambition had
taken place in his mind, in our imaginations, and in the
plans of his shrewd advisers. Trudeau himself remained
a man of passionate divisions and vindictive oppositions.
So his physical stature was small, but his belief in reason,
his hope for a population mature in its political-cultural
engagements was not. The size of his dream, his con-
tradictions, his ambitions, and his flippancy, fused in the
complexity of a man who declared war on us and never allowed us to touch him. Trudeau needed space, private and
public. The space of this country was open enough to run
an army of ideas and questions: those manifestos manifested in the years before he came to power, in prose that
presaged the use of power, and in stage poses that said,
"This is power." Modern politics, conditioned by electric
media and thriving on extremes of thrall and nausea, allowed no time for balanced insight. But this was certain: *la
guerre* was not a deadening affair. Choices were presented;
a meaning was demanded; an appeal to the imagination

was made; and admiration and hate were loosed. It was an education in passion.

When the time came for him to resign, he did so, with sly mythic timing, on February 29, 1984, a Thursday in a Leap Year. He spoke of looking for signs in the sky of his destiny while in the grip of the archetypal northern experience: a snowstorm.

Then the recall to Ottawa. Sixteen years: history and symmetry. And Pierre Trudeau alone in front of microphones, under high-voltage lamps, in the fantasia of televised politics.

MAGNETIC CITY

**WELCOME TO
PROGRESSIVE CONSERVATIVE
COUNTRY**
—a sign looming in the midst of the Turner compound.

Ottawa: it was a humid week in 1968 when the capital was the butt of innumerable jokes about being like a colonial village; where after midnight it was impossible to find decent restaurants open when the convention closed; where the highways leading in from Ontario to the capital were invariably under construction, incapable of handling huge volumes of traffic. ("What's the difference between yogurt and Ottawa?" Answer: "More culture in yogurt"— wit from a time capsule.) Now museum-like, British-style government centres became suddenly archaic while the surroundings surged up like Braque paintings in silver and steel. Without government, the city would be Bytown on the Rideau. With government, it was an experimental showpiece. Whole areas were refashioned, sandblasted, and renamed.

Rapid transit: across Canada, from Toronto to Calgary, a universal Magnetic City was being built. Ottawa had rushed from 1884 to 1984 in a decade and a half; and the young people's faces were unwrinkled, as eager and fresh as affluent graduates.

Midnight at the Ottawa Westin: a party for John Turner. Free of charge, if you were a delegate or an observer with friends on the inside, light beer, white wine, dope in the washrooms, and a thirty-second conversation with a Trudeau cabinet minister supporting Turner: "Hi, my name is...Hope you'll support us on the first ballot...."

"What's going on?" a lovely and leggy brunette from Winnipeg asked. She was blocked by a security guard and told it was the night of Trudeau's farewell. "Oh...him," she said.

Another security guard sipped beer and leered at female delegates. He fingered his belt radio and paused to pat the bulge over his belt.

"Yeah, dat guy, Trudeau, he'd make a great dictator," he said to my shock. "I know dat, eh? Yeah, I'd have voted for him again and again. Dat for sure."

After this history—what? There was no choice for one who wanted to examine universal states of ambiguity (USA). Find a description for the post-literate experience. Explore the milieu.

3

POLITICS IN THE AGE OF ANGELISM

Across the communications landscape
move the spectres of sinister technologies
and the dreams that money can buy.
J.G. Ballard

In the Age of Angelism—Jacques Maritain's metaphor
connoting the loss of the body, of the sense of the real,
what has been named Discarnate Man—who is in control is a concern of painful relevance. Behind the disputes
of the Trudeau decades, whether abortion, capital punishment, language rights, or Third World involvement—lie
the issues of responsibility and authority. The problem:
responsibility comes from a recognition of presence. Rational social action depends on agreed-upon contracts,
confirmation of contact. But what if there is less and
less contact between people? What if we are treated like
ghosts, shadows, gods, or devils? The result: we feel impotent (helpless, hopeless) or omnipotent (like supermen,
untouchable, monolithic). Victims and *Übermenschen*. As

people of the middle ground, we can recognize that the Canadian cultural obsession with victimization is the flip side of a belief in total superiority. This helps explain why literary nationalism produced Margaret Atwood's *Survival*. And it may be why the liberal democracies are experiencing "a serious crisis", in the words of the CBC National News. The effect of the Age of Angelism on politics is to force a return to mask and phantasmagoria. Issues dissolve; attention is on a politician's pose; orgasmic drives determine victories; media attention turns into cinema; reportage into gossip and opinion; people into stereotypes; debate and analysis into received opinion and spectacle. The words used to describe politicians and policies suggest etherealization: substantial or insubstantial, with matter or without. Thus gravity (focus) against weightlessness (out of focus, floating souls).

Trudeau had substance; therefore he was opaque, hard to see through. He understood that these are bad days for literate speech in the service of the good. The Irrational Rationalist had to manage his message from multiple angles. And Friday in the Civic Centre, other spirits were shaping perception.

Clouds of cliché trailed the occasion.

We had been here before. The convention was haunted by TV replays and literary descriptions of political gatherings, past, present, and future. Dallas and San Francisco were hosting the Republicans and the Democrats that summer too. But there was also a weird recurrence of 1968, an eerie feel of letdown and buildup. Who could succeed Trudeau and move the arena into rebirth?

Mood is mind. And in the days that followed the speeches (on Friday) and the voting (on Saturday), the mood turned anti-climactic. The journalists and the electric media conjured alternative spirits: to exorcize the familiar feeling there would have to be an excited simulation. For any writer, the conventions established by Mailer,

Vidal, and V.S. Naipaul made it difficult to find a new angle.

In the press room under the Exhibition Hall, I heard typewriters, TV sets, radios, and monitors, the whir and ripple of talk, feedout from terminals, gossip about bought delegates, payoffs and kickbacks, the vibration of innuendo. I watched images being traced. A face no longer mattered; polls and profiles provided the impetus for Saturday June 16, the Bloomsday of *Ulysses*, James Joyce's fictional day, June 16, 1904, of wandering and universal synchronicity.

Reporters and politicians both were tuned into global energy: computers and word-processors run by command centres in hotels or in mobile trucks, where experts via headphones discussed delegate tracking, targeting, and the Buddy System.

In the Civic Centre, TV cameras focused on pretty girls in red tunics: there were closeups of muscled dancer legs. Interviews were conducted with delegates. Along the aisles of TV sets in the press room, you could wander and watch. Voices in headsets emanated from booths. (Note: walkmans and headsets push the wearer inside, transforming the external world into pantomine; shut-off leads to shut-out; the inner world of solipsism, Big Brother residing within, not outside where he can be identified and resisted.) Commentators, saturated by the white light of studio-lamps, gazed out through glass. To me, with no access to the signals, the anchormen were pattering to...nothing.

Since identity was being so vaporized, I tried to read the candidates' names for the sign of something concrete. Turner, Johnston, Whelan, Roberts, Munro, MacGuigan. They weren't promising.

Yet insidious whisperings whirled around the unlikeliest name: Jean Chrétien, christian and cretin all rolled into one. No one is responsible in reporting rumour. But

Turner was disliked by the press. He was the Bay Street
Boy, the Man from Glad, Biff the Jock, the Ultimate Wasp
(though he is a Catholic, like Trudeau, Clark, Chrétien,
and Mulroney). Chrétien was the populist hero, and he had
something of a sexual interest for the cameras: a seductive
image. It did not matter that Chrétien after twenty years in
politics had to be, like Turner, a representative of Powerful
Concerns; Chrétien had been appointed the Street Fighter.
He was battered, balding, and inevitably described by the
cliché machine as looking like a punch-drunk old boxer.
Chrétien had been in the political game for a long time,
and he had no doubt "eaten too much plastic chicken",
as he said. But he was a shrewd person who could play
off a crowd. Turner was better in small groups. Chrétien
got revved up in front of the mass. Where Turner radiated blue-eyed paranoia on TV, Chrétien was ready with
his "I Love Canada" speech. Turner was too slow for the
cameras: hence conservative. Chrétien operated at the perfect speed: fast. Ostensibly, the issues involved were that
Turner belonged to the party's right wing and Chrétien was
the standard-bearer for Trudeau and the progressive left.
This was mostly a media fiction, but it made the event less
tedious. Trudeau had not declared his preference, but it
was understood that he had no use for John Napier Turner,
whose name was broadcasting Turncoat.

Friday: in the absence of a well-defined symbol like
Trudeau, the dominant word in the candidates' speeches
was "New". God was gone; Full Employment was the
deity of the day. Each speaker paid tribute to PET, who
looked down from above, in the stands. The banner-
phrases revolved around making things if not look New—
difficult for these exhausted politicians, inexplicably out

of training for the rigours of political grandstanding—then at least sound New.

Cynical aphorisms from the CBC personnel: "Whelan's outside warming up his mouth. He's eating a pig...." "MacGuigan. Yeah. Well, at least he won't shout. He might crack his face." On John Roberts's French: "Is he speaking German too?"

Trudeau had not encouraged genius in his cabinet; and the results of the one-man army were on painful display that night.

Saturday. On the way to the Civic Centre, a taxi driver said, "Yeah...different today. The Tories were always talkin' about how they were goin' to kill each other! Not here. Nice y'know? But Turner's got it....That's what the papers say...."

Switch in. Trudeau at the centre of a press scrum as he returned to his box (scrambling reporters trailed by people with booms and cords) and he gliding through as if oblivious (police, aides, and fans rushing him, trying to protect him or poke through) and Trudeau still contained and even serene (the scrum growing and seething, everyone eager for a quote or a shrug) and Trudeau not obliging them as he continued his way back through the crowd up to his seat in the stands.

THE ATMOSPHERE OF WORDS

The origin of breathing, however, lies in breathing.
Elias Canetti

"I see your pencil going there," the CBC man shook his head in honest shock, "and I wonder what century I'm in." As a Canadian writer, I'd often found myself asking that question too: just what century are we in? A critical perspective requires distance and solitude. To answer that question, I needed privacy to think. It wasn't possible to find any silence on the convention floor, except in the toilets; so I decided to observe the atmosphere of writing and reporting.

With the professional journalists, the words I heard were "interphase", "grid patterns", "networking", and "programming": concepts for the era of the word-processor and the computerized poll. Apparently, only a computer could keep track of the political velocity and hum. The printed word operated on lag-time; it could take months, even years, before a thoughtful and lengthy work on the event could be published.

Thus in the Age of Angelism, the writer's role is under pressure. If the audience is dissolving into post-literacy or retreating into academic cloisters (a captive public), then the attempt to find a radical grip on experience through words is plagued with problems of publication and readership. The screen and the electric hum have replaced the page and the pen. No one was sure of what the results would be. But you could identify certain effects: the focus on mood in writing, on weightlessness, on characters cut loose from the ground of experience.

The human mind depends on language to utter thought, to make thoughts outer. But how do you write about electricity, speed, invisibility, or music, when each is a non-verbal mode? If you were sentenced to the page, you were sentenced to use words to describe terminal activities. Word-processors flipped you into storage and retrieval, networks, impalpable sources, accelerated data. Perhaps this electric presence in literature was an explanation of the self-reflexive text: words as interiorized signs, and myths without any reader at all.

Of course, all writers can tell you about fiction and myth. But as Richard ("I misspoke myself") Nixon said: there are lies, and there are Lies. Truth is found in measuring the falsehoods and in the attempt to recover a reality from the blur of blurbs and bytes.

Trudeau had said *There is the danger that mass media constitute a vehicle for error.*

"What century are you in?"

The CBC man had raised the problem of Canadian writing itself: few challenge the political-social milieu we live in. Most have trouble believing that a social reality is there. The average novelist-poet-critic (each vocation distinct from the other; you must accept your box in the Great White North) stumbling in from the nineteenth-century bush, taught to detest North American society, having received the blessings of the Two Essential Grants (George and the Canada Council), after ripping out in record time (ten years) yet another work on the True Themes (bestiality and the Small Town)—well, you wouldn't expect those who claim that they don't do research to see that electric politics determine most of our social-cultural environment. The result: the habitual intellectual stance is remote from the scene's dynamics. A writer's protest is defused into a so-called civility or apathy. The institutions stay uncriticized, and the contract with the reader is betrayed.

The journalists who reported the event were strait-jacketed by editorial formats, membership in the press club, and by the corporations that were paying their bills. The press's cynicism was usually a disguise for self-loathing and fear. *I have never been able to read newspapers* [Trudeau said] *without a sense of uneasiness....They follow their customers and are therefore always lagging behind reality.*

There is little pleasure in attacking colleagues and cabals. "Everyone has to make a living...." "Compromises are the heart of the political life...." Sarcasm can be a cover for sorrow and frustration.

But if our investment is in truth, then an investigator will be drawn to people engaged in public manoeuvring. The question that came to the fore: who were the networks behind the rumours of bought delegates, the processors and polls, the mood of canvassing and tracking?

Insert edit. When Pope Paul II left Canada, on September 23, 1984, two days before Queen Elizabeth II arrived in New Brunswick, one day before Prime Minister Brian Mulroney arrived in Washington, DC, to seek closer ties with Ronald Reagan, this appeared in the *Toronto Star*:

IS CANADA HEADING FOR NEW FEUDALISM?

Then under the phrase "The Canadian Dynasties"

Over the past few years more and more Canadian companies have been gobbled up by small powerful families. Operating in virtual anonymity these families now control a vast network of the Canadian economy.

First paragraph

> ...control of Canada's economy is passing into the
> hands of the few...a new form of economic and political
> feudalism...a 20th-century version of Upper Canada's
> Family Compact back in the 1800s.

The article carried denials by the major players in
the Family Compact—Conrad Black, the Bronfmans, and
Paul Desmarais of Power Corp. The feature concerned
corporate influence, alliances based not on inherited priv-
ilege, but on banks and bucks. These Family Compacts
were the mystery agents at the Liberal and Conservative
conventions.

This was not the official news. Most in the press were
aware of the links; most chose to describe the spectacle
instead. The people who make the news sometimes depend on a Plain Reader who is numb and indifferent so
that events will slip by unnoticed. And Canadians have
replaced Americans as the fresh-faced *naïfs* of the New
World. We seem to be breathing in the twentieth century
as if for the first time.

Thus the concealed wiring of an electric event may only
be exposed when money power is traced to its *corp*.
Who can enter those spheres of influence? Few do. For
political power today has no real centre. It is impossible
to say that one source alone channels the force of the
political machine. It may be that "machine" is itself an
outmoded term. The New Feudalism is screened from
view, while the Old Feudalism was evident in pomp and
parade. (Note: an arranged marriage now occurs when the
son or daughter of a major candidate marries the son or
daughter of a chairman of the board.) On the street, black

limousines with tinted windows slide towards offices that resemble Victorian banks. Towering offices are built with window-mirrors. They can see out, but you can't see in. The architecture itself is a metaphor for hiding. Trails are left, traces like smells from the Cadillac's exhaust; but little can be directly tracked. Computers, telephones, and teletypes generate paranoia because their effect is to seem as if nobody is responsible for the influx of datamation. Ask the question "Who is in control?" of those who you suspect are the right people, and their reply is the inevitable denial: "We don't affect the political process." So the factions vanish. Into confusion, diffusion. Stateless money. International transfers. Corporate heads accountable to no one. Backroom plots. Uncontrollable mystery. Which is why cracking cabals and codes is the occult trade of the late twentieth century, and why writers from Wyndham Lewis and Marshall McLuhan to Norman Mailer and J.G. Ballard turned to culture, politics, and myth and found themselves on the apocalyptic edge of demonology and angelism. A literature of atmospherics is the portrayal and critique of mood and mind. The nihilism in our time: when the ephemeral becomes the absolute nothing can be remembered, and being itself seems to evaporate into

CONVENTION AIR

In the rather likely event that you no longer have the faintest notion of who I am, allow me to introduce myself once again: My name is Franz Kafka...
Letters to Felice

...the dancing and chanting in the arena—"CRET-chen...CRET-chen...CRET-chen...CRET-chen..." alternating with "TURN-ner...TURN-ner..." and, in weaker tones, "John-SON...John-SON..."—the space smelling like cigarettes and cigars and spilled coke....

"Will Chrétien win on the third ballot?" asked a girl with a blue-and-white hat.

"Sure," the CBC man said.

"How," said a Turner supporter in an orange-gold smock, "when we need just a hundred and fifty votes to win the second ballot?"

The CBC man shrugged. "Hey. Chrétien is great copy."

Zeitgeist sounds: *the politics of dancing...the politics of...mmm looking good...the politics of moving...it's a message understood...*I recalled that song while popular pieces hummed in the background; "What a Feeling" from *Flashdance* being a favourite.

Rock-'n'-roll conventions: in 1968, there had been brass bands, jazz groups, and plump lady singers from New Brunswick; now there were tapes, compact discs, radios, and auditorium speakers. Glenn Gould had said that we would be surrounded by pre-recorded sonic fields. In *The Glenn Gould Reader*, he writes of his sensitivity to breathing and heat like a media-val alchemist terrified of the demons the dark breathes out. He says that the appropriate atmosphere is essential for audio broadcast and reception. Over the two days in Ottawa, Platinum Blond and the Powder Blues Band played at candidates' parties; contenders were heralded with Van Halen ("Jump"), Vangelis ("Chariots of Fire"), and synthesizers and guitars overloading the amplifiers to the point of distortion...*the politics of dancing...*When you want to manipulate mood, use rock 'n' roll. It's a way to manage movement and deflect attention away from who is working the controls....*the politics of...mmmmmm looking good...*We had been so thoroughly musicked that the mere downbeat from a familiar tune shot us into euphoria....

On the slippery floor littered with cups, pop tins, and discarded signs (Whelan, Munro, MacGuigan), young men and women danced and sang in cheering sections…"Hel-lo John! Bye Bye Mull-rooney"…*it's a message understood*…

Something reformulated after Trudeau's farewell. But what? No one dared air premonitions. Around Turner's section, on the west side of the building, journalists jostled and waited. Around Chrétien's box on the east side, closer to Quebec, the mood was subdued. A feeble joke: "What'ya call someone who knocks over an outdoor toilet?…a john turner." And in the stands, Trudeau demonstrated his command of spatial power. He forced those on the floor to constantly look up to see what he was doing.

Turner 1,862…Chrétien 1,368…Johnston 192…

While Turner came to the podium, Trudeau met with each defeated candidate and paused for a moment with Chrétien. History would say this was a farewell: in fact Chrétien's political career was to end that day; within two years, he would have retired from public view. Then Trudeau turned and did not introduce the Prime Minister-elect. He stood back on the platform, hands folded in a self-defence judo posture, his sharp eyes stabbing into the backs of the speakers, a shy—sly?—smile on his lips. Trudeau presented a perfect paradoxical picture: wonder and ruthlessness.

After Chrétien spoke, provoking with off-the-cuff passion an emotional response from the crowd. Turner approached the microphones, cleared his throat, and addressed the assembly. Dead air came over the hall. Applause was slack. "People are just tired," a cameraman muttered. "It doesn't mean anything." But it did.

The only constant factor in my thinking over the years has been opposition to accepted opinions.

With his silence on stage, Trudeau returned to his natural state: *opposition to accepted opinions*. The Liberal

Party would lose the election and would have to rebuild from the beginning; Turner himself would have to contend with the memory of civil war. That night, Trudeau stood out: still the centre; speaking with his posture.

To "ready-made" or second-hand ideas, I have always preferred my own.

In the packed halls when I left, I heard at my back the amplifiers sending out their murky electronic call.

4

LA GUERRE EST FINIE

A mask expresses much, but hides even more.
Above all it separates.
Elias Canetti

Shirtsleeves rolled up, suspenders snapped tight to hold up his pants, stomach bulging over his belt, Senator Keith Davey emerged from his office in East Block, the Parliament Buildings, acknowledging me with a glance and a wave and: "Can you wait a minute?" And I was struck by his resemblance to Willie Stark in Robert Penn Warren's *All the King's Men*—rather, of his striking resemblance to Broderick Crawford in Robert Rossen's film. Here was a former kingpin: the embodiment of backroom power; he was the echo of his work, networking made flesh. After time, people look like their professions. Shrewd and pragmatic, Senator Davey was reputed to be a master of management, the field man for Liberal governments. Looking like Willie Stark—big, formidable, and secure enough to be careless about dress—certainly couldn't hurt. "Come in, now," he said, his hand stuck out for the perfunctory shake. "Sit down." He motioned at two couches facing each other on either side of a low coffee table. "I want to...have a good look at you."

I was manoeuvred to a place on the couch in the sun. Davey settled in with his back to the window; sprawled in a dishevelled pose, the Senator could have a very good view, with the sun behind him shining like a spotlight on my face. I couldn't return his gaze without blinking, squinting, or shielding my eyes.

Davey, to my surprise, shut his eyes. I hadn't expected his genial cornpone appearance. But he wasn't asleep. He was taking me in, evaluating. Then he smiled and said in a low voice, "What do you want?"

"To see Trudeau."

A raised eyebrow.

"Why?"

To discuss certain issues through dialogue. I emphasized I didn't want an interview.

For ten minutes I was grilled, probed, held up, and revolved as if I were an object taken from a display case and examined with a view to the possibility of purchase. Pleasantries, courtesies, questions. "What sort of political writers do you admire?"...Mailer? Yes. (Davey had a hardback copy of *Tough Guys Don't Dance* on the coffee table.) Vidal? Yes.

He glanced off. His hands slid up and down his suspenders. I almost expected to hear a southern accent from him. *Naw lissen heah, buoy.*

Instead, he spoke amiably. "Well now I'm a strategist...a political tactician. I'm interested in giving advice on power. I wouldn't presume...[here he gazed at the ceiling] to try and *joust* with Trudeau. However...[his eyes dropped down] if you want to see him [he leaned forward, his voice descending the register] it could be arranged...."
A wait for effect.

Professional politicians speak cryptically. If you don't understand the messages, you are worse than dead: you're an amateur, probably a mere voter. Senator Davey relished his role: the insider's mask. His apparent lack of attentiveness was expertly done. He could observe without appearing to soak anything up. By the time I left, I had the feeling I'd been thoroughly absorbed.

I cleared my throat.

"What's Trudeau doing these days?"

"He works at his law firm in Montreal. It's basically a PR job. People drop by and take him out for lunch. He's also teaching his children...Latin."

Why, I wondered: so that they can read Virgil in the original?

It was impossible to imagine Trudeau retired, shunning the public arena he had rigorously dominated. But I thought: what if you meet him and find a man fishing? Retirement has its masquerades too. If Trudeau had turned solitary, his silence as eloquent as a shrug, there was a reason for it.

"I'll contact you next week," Davey said, "after I see him...."

June 1985: three weeks before, Prime Minister Mulroney's first budget had been tabled in the House of Commons; three weeks later premiers René Lévesque and Peter Lougheed (sparring partners during *la guerre civile*) would resign from office; and Pierre Trudeau, activist of reason, was in self-imposed exile in his Corbusier Monastery of Art on Avenue des pins in Montreal.

In 1986: books, books, books....They rolled off the press about the Trudeau years: self-aggrandizing memoirs, historical analyses, sentimental justifications, journalistic reports, anecdotal hints, and oral autobiographies. The oral culture produces a flow of rumour: word of mouth pushes up conspiracy theory, suspicion, paranoia. When there is the absence of hard fact, we find a flood of whispers, speculations, hints, and exaggerations: the creations of myth. Everyone from Keith Davey in *The Rainmaker* (Reignmaker or Reinmaker) to Jean Chrétien in *Straight from the Heart* contributed to the influx with apologies, fictions, and narratives. And through it all, Trudeau, the object of fascination, remained "unavailable for comment".

In whatever private agenda Trudeau had set for himself, his resistance to surveillance by electric media provoked an urge to complete his image through books and articles. But in the aftermath of his dream, we had been pressed into new political configurations: Mulroney's machinations, a Government Corporation ruled by the bodiless unreality of polls; hence a government without an idea, and hence inviting collapse.

VISIBLE, INVISIBLE

"Tides" have names.
Wyndham Lewis

If the arbiters of the post-literate status quo are the electronic media, then we should recall how John Turner's political life foundered on TV. It was not the notorious "I Had No Choice" debate of July 25, 1984, when Mulroney had Turner pinned against the wall over the patronage deals with Trudeau. It was during the dialogue of the masks, August 15, the Women's Debate, featuring the three party leaders. Turner was tired; his suit was creased; his speech was choked, as if he couldn't breathe and he was under water; his face twisted into peculiar contortions. You could only guess at the thoughts of this man who had been a cabinet minister, a once-and-former prime minister, if only he were patient (according to Lester B. Pearson). That evening Turner appeared almost human, framed by microphones, one-minute clips, and talking heads. On TV, Turner had been slashed off at the waist, and all that we saw was a face in pain.

Unlike Trudeau, Turner needed the current going for him. He had misread the patterns and polls. Trudeau's presence was still the currency; reaction had set in ("change for its own sake..."). Turner hadn't understood the tide of his time, and when the TV current rose against him, he sank. It would take two years for him to resurface in opposition.

Mulroney was already prime minister, the polls told him: he didn't have to do anything in the debate; so he didn't. The ultimate insider, with no private identity, it hardly mattered if Mulroney was real. Technocratic society had taken the entire post-World War II period to incubate this perfect specimen. His name in Irish slang— Mull-rooneyed, means to be conned. We would later discover the truth of his name in Quebec slang: *Mal-runné*, to run something badly.

The TV spectacle charged on.

Tuesday, September 4, 8:45 p.m.: the reporters' clichés announced "the end", and down the Trudeau Party went, ministers and aides and friends. TV journalists enthusiastically slurred their words and made "massive dissolution" sound like "mass-if-disillusion". 1:00 a.m: Prime Minister-elect Mulroney appeared with his wife, Mila, in a hockey arena in Mulroney's home town of Baie Comeau. The delirious crowd crowed Bry-N...with applause that sounded like static. Mila hugged Bry-N's shoulder, reading his notes to herself, hovering close to her husband so that she could nudge him if he started to drone or dither. But this was Bry-N's one night in the arena, and the electrician's son was not about to blow it. And what did the winner of the most powerful majority in Canadian history say? No one remembers. In the House of Commons, Mulroney would seem distracted, abstracted, even during another scandal that involved his government; his meetings with the press were infrequent, as if he were trying out a vanishing act, his voice so low and slow you had to strain to pay attention.

Mulroney wanted to practise the art of media management. Like Trudeau, he sensed the possessive powers that be (become) in the Age of Angelism. Unlike Trudeau, he could not transcend the cameras and tape recorders and speak to others; nor did he demand that the Plain Citizen read the issues and images for himself. But the TV camera had turned x-ray, and the Plain Citizen could see through him.

CHARTER OF RITES

"Aren't you some sort of communist?"
Trudeau: "No, I'm a canoeist."
Gloss: "I early realized that ideological systems
were the true enemies of freedom."

Noon in Montreal, September 1985. Fourteenth floor, 1001 Boulevard de Maisonneuve Ouest. Law firm of Heenan Blaikie Jolin Potvin Trepanier Cobbett. Receptionists murmuring into headphones; glass doors separating you from inner offices; to the right, a large spiral staircase.

I waited, settled into a velvet couch, half expecting Pierre Trudeau to descend the staircase. It had taken time to get here through letters, phone calls, and mild persuasion. And the soft surroundings of the legal office seemed too reverent a place to meet the former PM.

Suddenly a voice well known to me from a thousand TV and radio broadcasts said my name from the left, the direction of the toilets and elevators. I turned to see Trudeau, dressed in an open-neck yellow shirt and creased slacks, coming towards me. Panic. I had worn a new suit.

"So, where are we going for lunch?" Trudeau asked, his eyes amused. His manner was shrewdly upsetting: the casual dress and entrance from the left had given him an extra edge. But it was time to go outside.

On the street, passers-by gawked at Trudeau; cars screeched, horns honked, people paused on the sidewalk.

"We'll have to find some place," Trudeau said (he had by now put on a light jacket with a rose in the lapel), "where people won't want to shake my hand or give me hell."

He stopped in front of a hole-in-the-wall Vietnamese restaurant.

"This is a place," he gestured, "where the businessmen take their mistresses. Of course, I never do."

Inside it was dark, narrow, nearly empty.

"Is this all right?" he asked. At the back, we were not disturbed. Then we talked in the dimly lit place: we moved from politics to humanism in the technological society, to rationality—"balance and proportion"—and on to charting social transformations. "Yes," Trudeau said, "the whole map has changed."

"Rational politics," he said. "The ordinary person can be appealed to through common sense. Beyond the effects of technology. My grandfather, for instance, was not especially literate but he was able to reason choices out...what proposals Wilfrid Laurier was making. I believe you can speak directly to that spirit of choice." When a direct statement was posed, Trudeau would snap straight in his

seat. Erect; serious; eyes concentrated. I almost expected
a sting of retaliation. But a savage swerve in his mood
never occurred. Occasionally there were distractions from
the waitress (she was shaken by serving Trudeau); inter-
ruptions with arrival of food (no wine; we drank water).
Sometimes Trudeau would lean across the table to listen
closely to a question, as if he were straining to catch the
words.

On his writings: "I have a preference for the polemical.
But I won't write my memoirs. Too many are doing that."
Too narcissistic? "Yes. Narcissistic. But I like a good fight.
I can't say I'm interested in discussing my past. Though I
suppose if I did, it would run to 12,000 pages." The conversation covered the constitution and the debates of those
years ("There were many disappointments...especially
with the charter,"), the fate of democracy in post-literacy
("Is there any indication that because you are literate,
you'll be aware?"), associations of ideas emerging. "I tried
to read everything until I entered politics...." Trudeau
spoke of preparations, training for a long-term run. "Reason is not logic. It's been misinterpreted that way. I'm
an intensely passionate person...." Admissions and omissions: he was conscious of his effect, but there was an
intensity of ideas behind his statements. "There are many
fine journalists; but what I have distrusted is the arrogance
they show in mediating between issues and people. They
are another power group holding sway in society as a
whole."

The question of face: close up, Trudeau was strangely
shaped. In profile: the sculpted oriental look. There was
a tautness about him: not a brittle edge, but a tense poise
that recalled his prose of twenty years before. He professed
relaxation. But I could not believe his rite of retirement
was permanent.

"Rumour": from the Latin *rumorem* and the nominative *rumor*, meaning a noise, a murmur; *rumitare*, "to spread reports"; from the base *rum*, a buzzing sound (distant relative: "rumble"). In our musicalized circumstance of echo and playback, overtones swirl around any figure in the current. Before this lunch with Trudeau, like crazed circuits, the currents had buzzed.

"So you're seeing the Man," a publisher acquaintance said on the telephone. "Good. I gotta question for him."

What? My friend was normally calm and reasonable.

"Ask him...if he administered drugs to Maggie to engineer those Christmas births!...What timing. Just a coincidence?...Ask him about those Swiss bank accounts. Ask him about his plot to cook up a French Catholic takeover of the government...stocking Ottawa with his henchmen. Ask him *that*!"

Another worried about Trudeau's stand on abortion in 1967; one worried about his visceral side; another insisted that I inquire if Reagan had been killed in the assassination attempt and a robotoid put in his place.

In the Age of Angelism, irrational fears emanate from people who receive all broadcasts but who can not filter out the generations of secret news. We become obsessed about the body when we are uncertain about reality itself.

"I'd be paralysed," a friend who admired Trudeau said. "What would you say to him?...He's over six feet tall y'know....And that intelligence. It's scary."

I remembered these exchanges while the gracious "beast" on the other side of the table ate strawberries for dessert and continued to talk: "Richard Nixon was a complex man. Full of self-doubts....Very strange. But even without Kissinger he would have had a shrewd appraisal of global politics....Reagan has the talent to sense the direction of the crowd and place himself in the front. He has a strong feeling for the movement of affairs. But he's not my kind of politician."

These statements, I realized in retrospect, told me only as much as Trudeau wanted me to know. This was inevitable. A round followed of random and rough opinions of politicians, provincial and federal, of colleagues and issues. "The 'Northern *Magnus*'...the gunslinger...the press likes a show," he said. Because Trudeau had experienced the constraints of office, he had not been able to read many books. "Who should I read?" He was curious about Glenn Gould: "What were his politics?" They had never met ("If he had lived in Montreal...") His interests ranged from movies like *Apocalypse Now* to Kurtz and the dilemma of the humanist faced with irrationality. He asked about historical revisions of the views of Nixon and Vietnam.

Lunch over (he paid), he paused to shake hands with the cook and the waitress: the professional politician practising his trade. The impression of him: sharp articulation; energy; and a well-guarded self. Also a man whose agenda was completed. This politician who had often chosen not to act like one was determined to chart his own destiny.

"A Law may be made to bind All the Subjects of a Commonwealth: A Liberty, or Charter is only to One Man, or some One part of the people," Thomas Hobbes writes in "Of Commonwealth", Part II, Chapter 26 of *Leviathan*. To chart is to document routes for travelling so that another person will not get lost. A Charter of Rights is a legal document, cast in impenetrable jargon, that charts for the individual the possibility of navigating in alien waves. A charter is long-term travel, politically instituted, to assist in pointing out rights and obligations.

Yet listen to other overtones in "chart". Because name, character, and presence concern us, a charter of rights can assume the part of metaphorical blueprint. Everyone a potential cartographer, mapping landscapes and soundscapes, alert to assaults on integral self.

A bright afternoon; and people strolling.

Trudeau eased out in front of me to flirt with two statuesque Montreal women. They stepped back and tittered when they recognized the diminutive man who teased them.

On Maisonneuve.

"*Monsieur le Prime Ministre*," a voice called. "When are you coming back?"

Trudeau waved.

"I'm not," he said.

And—smiling—he disappeared into the Aetna building, glass doors shutting behind him.

5

BIOGRAPHY OR HISTORY

Where there is no strain, there is no history.
Collingwood

When future writers assess Trudeau's crafty spirit, will it be through biography and myth—his, and individualized—or through history—ours, and generalized? We attempt clarity in the midst of celebrity imagery. *If you move quickly enough, no one can define you*—the statement has (strange thing) been attributed on occasion to Trudeau, McLuhan, and Gould. The emphasis in that sentence is surely on "quickly": in the sense of "with life". Of these three men, only Trudeau chose the role of historical confrontation. He dragged Canadians into the twentieth century and closer to the American style of presidential republicanism. The hazards are enormous. It is impossible to know if Canadians have the tenacity and toughness to survive in the modern state, with its invisible fields and accelerated tempi, its magnetic media and their polarities of terror and trash. Trudeau challenged us with what we had never before truly encountered: the force of myth, multiplicity, ambiguity. Yes, the spirit of the age is ambiguity. But we were unprepared for his agenda; we were unaware; we preferred and prefer docility and dollars. And Trudeau threw himself unwillingly—one of his convenient covering fictions (there must always be drama)—into the mild life of a northern nation that almost but not quite existed, and provoked the moral storm. He wrote his own script, created a public mask and stage, then acted out the part and persona of the age he had helped to initiate. Trudeau was, over his sixteen years as leader, the most implacable visionary the place without a face had yet produced. He was selective in his attention. He was aristocratic, rude, aloof. He demanded we not accept ourselves as the dispassionate passengers of history. He projected the possibility of an independent line—lucid, elusive, sometimes reclusive, analytical, critical, and engaged.

History, dream, fiction, myth. They are treacherous words. "A man is nothing without a dream," the cliché goes; but the obverse of the dream of reason is the technocratic nightmare. Modern history is haunted by the spectacle of soured vision, of those political and electronic Utopians who threatened to rearrange and then derange our fragile grasp, what Milan Kundera calls our "unbearable lightness of being." All a writer can do is question and warn. Any politician who urges us to reach beyond ourselves is suspect. Any politician who relies on charisma must incite skepticism.

Will those future judges treat Trudeau as a narrow intellectual, a man too solitary and single-minded to be sensitive to what the people were? Or will they regard him as Canada's first and perhaps last political-intellectual mystic? His era raises more questions than I can answer.

Trudeau himself was not simply a social and political phenomenon. He went public to defy, and remains as private and unresolvable as the strains he manifested. Perhaps that is what he intended: the unsettled condition. So we are left tensed. Thinking: aside from the legacy of language rights and constitutional challenge, of deficits and divisiveness, we still do not comprehend the accomplishments of his regime. He may have been too long an expert in intangibles.

Yet there is no going back. *The universe is unfolding as it should.* Whatever history chooses to concoct about our time, it will surely say: this was the fierce growing up. *But we will dream some more.* Yes, we are going to have to dream. For the age that swung between energy and apathy, cynicism and hope, was for only one moment focused and fuelled by the fool and the fox, Pierre Elliott Trudeau.

A
SEARCH
FOR
GLENN
GOULD

1

MESSAGES

When Glenn Gould died, October 14, 1982, his reviews, conversations, and polemics were scattered in magazines and journals. I myself had kept track of his writings through a clippings file. These pieces were in no particular order and were disconnected in the styles and voices Gould used to lure or offend. Even in this format, his literary work had a vital and mysterious air that made me hunger to put the gatherings into an intelligible whole.

Then there was Gould himself: the recluse of St. Clair Avenue. I had grown up listening to him on the radio, watching his CBC-TV programs while he was performing and analysing (and endlessly explaining) Bach and Strauss (Richard). His brash opinions and odd appearances—sweaters buttoned up in disorderly fashion; cap and scarf and gloves in summer heat; adopted personae like Theodore "Ted" Slotz, the New York Cab Driver (doing Brando, doing Dean), Karlheinz Klopweisser, and Sir Nigel Twitt-Thornwaite, "the Dean of

British Conductors"—made him irresistible material for the myth machines.

And the myths multiplied: Gould arriving at midnight at a twenty-four-hour "coffee-and-donut" shop (I imagined a story: Gould dressed in an overcoat; July— it is steamy and close; street people sulk over coffee and doughnuts that taste like sugared paper; and one of the premier interpreters of Bach discoursing on Wagner, tape edits, and Thomas Mann's post-war novels); Gould driving his Lincoln over gravel roads in the dark, his hands sensuously feeling the steering wheel so that he could be close to the vibrations; Gould crooning Mahler *Lieder* to giraffes at the Metro Zoo; Gould driving his motorboat in circles on the lake near his cottage to scare away fish from fishermen; his love for Holiday Inns, shopping malls, radio, and TV; his friendship with Marshall McLuhan (I imagined another story: Gould arriving at 3 Wychwood Park to discuss communicable things, and the two saying nothing to each other); his refusal to perform in public; his choice of "the womb-like" recording studio; his night calls that interrupted others' sleep to become arias…improvisations… marathons.…

Then the irony of his recordings. He began in 1955 with a firm, fast version of *The Goldberg Variations*, and he finished in 1982 with a slower, meditative interpretation of the same music. The architecture seemed prearranged. But Gould, like McLuhan, believed in clarity and ratio, in the Great Bass or communicating line of music and thought. He was the rarest of things: a serious artist. His life assumes a pattern like variations, of themes stated and expanded, now resolved.

2

TRACKING

Then *The Glenn Gould Reader* and Jonathan Cott's *Conversations with Glenn Gould* (1984) remind us that for the serious artist nothing can be resolved. There are tensions under the surface of his trackings, dark notes to be reheard.

Consider him from other angles of possibility.

A boy huddled in thick coats like blankets eludes his friends. He has nothing in common with their antics. He has experienced their gentle jibes and misunderstandings. "Don't touch me," he thinks: "I'm different." Despising obscenity and humiliation, he withdraws into a mental stage: his imagination, free of power strictures and impositions. He identifies with animals: they are easily hurt, in need of protection, creatures that often resort to camouflage if they are to outwit hunters, trappers, and stockers of zoos. A photograph (1949) shows the youth at a piano with his dog: it is a comic pose, with the dog, Nicky, preparing to join in a duet. At an early age the boy cultivates a preference for heat, privacy, and insulation. At an early age he is called "genius".

However, his gift for musical and literary articulation is so sensational that audiences cannot help but want to touch him. Gloves become armour, scarves a protection, hats a mask, each article telegraphing "Do not disturb," but notice me. His harmless eccentricity resembles Mark Twain's taste for spotless white suits, his distaste for dust and dirt. Beware: take steps to insure insularity. The air is full of enemies. Transmittable germs. Severe measures may be required to bear the insidious surroundings.

Gossip hints at the artist's susceptibilities.

A handshake ruined him for weeks...He had to practise after he shook hands with someone...

He was polite...but the world was always seen through his eyes...

He wanted to be an uncaused cause...

The prodigy's accomplishments were exhilarating. "Listening to him on stage was like listening to how music should be played," an eyewitness said. Stage fright could be combatted with a variety of drugs. "Take three of these and you will go on stage saying 'Oh, you lucky people,'" Gould advised pianist William Aide. There is controversy, attendance. He is under constant inspection. His audiences not only listen; they observe.

At the peak of his performing popularity the virtuoso retires. He is thirty-two. The reaction: bewildered. There was more to come. Later Gould would confess his dislike of air-conditioning, airplanes, most cities, except for Toronto. However: "I could live a very productive life in Leningrad," he commented. "On the other hand, I'd have a crack-up for sure if I were compelled to live in Rome or New York." The press gives pressure; touring is up-rootment; the concert circuit plugs you into the racket and rush of adulation and cliques; streets seethe with dangers; pleasure in sensual attachments—the celebrity track, the sexiness of star life—is irrelevant to the pitch of energy he desires.

Gould announces his love for private glens, for wintry and crisp weather, for spaces untouched and untouchable. Action is rejected: meditation is encouraged. Only music matters.

More musings interpret him.

He was always unsatisfied with the cosmos as it is...

He was utterly solipsistic...

...utterly generous...

...always spinning people into his own web...he made people into myths...that they could never hope to live up to...

Gould makes new appearances in music magazines. Words expound, theorize, test. His articles read like manifestos, pleas, tracts. Suggestion: he wishes to become a new messenger-conductor, be the perfect communicator. So Gould lives on the printed page and on the air through recordings and the radio. He lives in the air in an apartment. (Visitors say his place was a mess.) His favourite city grows around him, experiencing transformation. Toronto is called the City of the Future: it's the city of the global antenna (the CN tower), mirrors, money, and fads. Within a decade, the city expands to global status. A neighbour of Gould's is the media expert who from the heart of the same city announces that the world is a village resonant with tribal drums.

Soon, as if Gould is playing a vampire, he goes out mostly at night. He drives a big American car, with the security of steel, glass, and metal plating. He uses the cover of darkness. (At night everyone is disguised.) He practises at home in the company of radios, TVs, and vacuum cleaners, every instrument switched on while he perfects the accents of a piece. From the other side of his receiving centre, electric instruments are conducted into vibrations, quavers, and quivers. All communication is drawn into a common destination: him.

He'd read a score first in his head. Memorize it all before playing. It would be alive in his mind before he ever touched the keys...

He took to phoning me....Odd hours....And he'd talk and talk....How could you hang up on Glenn Gould?...Things would sort of fade out when the monologue became a dialogue...

Geoffrey Payzant's *Glenn Gould: Music and Mind* is published in 1978. The book reads like a synoptic view, a timid critique of peculiar behaviour ("Talking Nonsense on Anything Anywhere"), and an over-awed testament to genius. It is reviewed in a Toronto newspaper by Gould: his answer to his advocate, keeping the call and response within a controlled range.

But Gould had an iconoclastic wit that ruptured a potentially precious solemnity. He cued us into play: his masks and stances put us on; we were to be his accompanists, sharing "in the spirit of the thing".

I once asked myself...What did Bach hum to himself when composing?...Then I noticed that when Gould played Bach he seemed to be humming something else to himself. It was not the piece he was actually playing. You see it became like a sort of double spiritual comment...All playing simultaneously. Like counterpoint...

What you heard when he played Bach wasn't Bach. It was Gould. A brand new music. "The Two-Part Inventions"...brought to you by Glenn Gould!...Sure...I enjoyed it. But would anyone have paid that much attention if his name hadn't been on the record sleeves?...

Push the angles on. Risk a contrast. Gould's cloakings echo another notorious recluse, Howard Hughes. The billionaire lived in antiseptic isolation, a lover of hotel rooms. He dictated demands through telecoms, teletypes, and telephones. ("Telephone": a voice from a distance.) He moved briefly to Vancouver because he had discovered what he believed was the secret of Canada: here you could be anonymous, yet here you could have international penetration.

Hughes ran and reran one movie for himself, *Ice Station Zebra* directed by John Sturges (director of *The Great Escape* and *The Satan Bug*, the latter about chemical warfare). *Ice Station Zebra* stars Rock Hudson (first celebrity to succumb to a disease that preys on immune deficiency) and Patrick McGoohan (star of *The Prisoner*; also the pharmacist in David Cronenberg's *Scanners*). In the movie an American nuclear submarine smashes up through Arctic ice to retrieve a downed space capsule that is being hunted by Soviet paratroopers—a small army that is dropped like propaganda leaflets from transport planes. On an artificial set meant to stand for the polar north, there is a contained East/West conflict: a confrontation over a surveillance device. During Hughes's period of movie watching (is he the forerunner of home video addicts?) his financial empire experienced unprecedented growth. He gained admittance to presidents. He was linked to the CIA and the FBI. He aided those scanners who specialize in monitoring others but who elude monitoring themselves. Howard Hughes went public only in death.

Then a shrunken ragman with tangled hair and filthy fingernails was exposed to the media light, a ghoulish figure grown from a pure hotel cell.

(Note: at Graceland Elvis Presley lived out another kind of communications' addiction—TV sets were left on, suffusing his home with a permanent background of white noise; remote-control cameras fed back images of bedrooms and bathrooms; walls were inlaid with hi-fi speakers, adding a further cushion of pop sound; and when the superstar flew to Las Vegas on a jet painted to resemble Air Force I, he landed, as if to confirm a symbolic link, at the private air terminal of Howard Hughes.)

We shouldn't push these coincidences to the point of absurdity. Hughes, however, personified the selfish technological mentality: the surveillance man. He was a voyeur in a diabolical nerve centre, holding others under his watchful eye. No longer human, he wanted to control his surroundings absolutely.

This selfishness would have been anathema to Gould. His recording of Bach's *Prelude and Fugue in C, No. 1*, from Book Two of the *Well-Tempered Clavier*, was included on the disc pressed for Voyager II: a quest for life, a request for answers from out there. When Gould's recordings were packaged for those earthbound, his touch was in evidence. His gifts were not used to savage others. His music came through, from stereo speakers and in headphones, from mass-produced tracks, in a selfless generosity.

Over the years, Gould's keyboard transcriptions and translations became elaborate. For some listeners, they were erratic; for others, irritating. Jonathan Cott's *Conversations* lists more than 150 entries, *The Glenn Gould Reader* more, citing Anhalt, through Taneiff (S.) to Wagner (R.). Gould engaged each piece as if for the first time, hiring musicians to try his account of old pieces, re-examining compositions already recorded by other virtuosi. What made critics hostile was his tempi. It was as if, while Gould taped, he was slowing each moment down or unexpectedly speeding up, tracking down undetected figures and intervals, hearing contrapuntal and contradictory voices, "splicing together...tape fragments", sensing stress that no one had traced, arcane ground few had tapped, "to approach the work...as it has never been heard before."

Still, his obsession: space, rehearing, and touch. Still, his concern: make the tradition new.

...there was a way of communicating something [Gould wrote] *no matter what, one person to another, while not being in the same room, in the same acoustical area...*

...the inner ear of the imagination is very much more a powerful stimulant than is any outward observation...

Behind Gould's investigations and commentaries came contrary desires.

I would very much like to take off for about a year to some frontier experience...spend a winter in the dark...

These contrary desires indicate a split in Gould. He seemed to speak in a secretive code that signified an inner/outer conflict. Through the cracks in his divided self, we see him both shutting himself off from the world (protecting his privacy) and struggling to stay public. For the one who is most responsive to life is often the one who is most sensitive to that life. The openness insures awareness; it also insures a risk. "The fear of being touched," Canetti says on the first page of *Crowds and Power*, is what allows an individual to feel separate: there is the fear of being absorbed into a crowd. To fear touch is to respect individual identity. T.E. Lawrence (of Arabia) had a dread

of shaking hands with others. And Gould must have realized: the responsiveness that makes you unique is the same
sensitivity that can kill you.

*I heard him on what turned out to be his last tour...years
ago....And he was amazing...But those mannerisms on
stage...bothered people. They thought he was excessive...fussy... irritating. Some said they'd never go to
see him again. They didn't want to be put off....I found
that...so strange...*

3

QUIRK QUOTIENT

In Gould's books, we encounter his taste for words. Avoidance and resistance: the more he wrote, the more he kept hidden. Yet literature is an acceptable field of creation and destruction. And words moved for him. Tim Page has repaged Gould's writings and gathered everything together that is publishable in *The Glenn Gould Reader*. He has arranged the essays into thematic order. They are grouped around headings like "Prologue", "Music", "Performance", an interlude where "g.g. interviews G.G. about Glenn Gould", "Media and Miscellany". All the familiar pieces from magazines and journals are here: "The Search for Petula Clark", "Stokowski in Six Scenes", "Streisand as Schwarzkopf", "The Idea of North"; the liner-notes for *The Goldberg Variations* and *The Art of the Fugue*; reviews of biographies of Mahler and Schoenberg; his polemics against Chopin and the later Mozart. Iconoclastic quotables cluster in the interviews: "If I hear another bar of the *Eroica,* I'll scream"; Mozart's "G-minor Symphony consists of eight remarkable measures... surrounded by a half-hour of banality." There are philosophical reflections on recording techniques and the studio; assaults on Stravinsky; apologies for Schoenberg.

I was surprised by the *Reader*. Once again I noted the dexterity of Gould's literary style, and the subtlety of his tone. He never saw a volume through publication. He was content to leave his writings in fragments. For an artist who spent a lifetime rethinking everything that had to do with music, this is startling. For *The Glenn Gould Reader* shows that, with his passing, we lost not only a fine musician and controversial presence but an essayist of wit and daring. His essays challenge the Plain Reader and, in an unexpected way, profoundly disturb.

Gould's essays open up his prose to the play of rhetoric, a flexibility of forms. This reflects his musical search for accurate, unforgettable communication. When forms are intersecting, interrupting each other, and essays read like novels and novels read like essays, it is the malleability of prose that gives it exciting promise for contemporary writing. (Milosz: "the neat division between novel, story, poetry, and essay is no longer clearly maintained.") It is my pet conceit, though, that prose in Canada is sadly undistinguished. There is no prose line established in the same vein as poetry; there are few models for the probing intellectual. Even Gould himself, with typical oversight by the Canadian literary establishment, is not treated as a literary person. There are of course many articulate musician-writers, like R. Murray Schafer and Alfred Brendel. But Gould wanted to be remembered as an intellectual; and his audience was fascinated by his waves of ideas. For those who apply their literacy in the late twentieth century are strangers in a strange land, indulging in what Gould calls "the Quirk Quotient".

Peculiar things happen when you are literate. You have an assumed analytical ability that lends a critical distance and clarity to your view. You are given a stand; and you also, abruptly, have the ability to snap your audience into some participatory stance. Essay prose can serve this tactical function of managing the reader's attention—which has, these days, the approximate concentration span of a gnat. But for prose to serve this function, whether in fiction or the essay, it must have

— a vital language
— a cultivated audience
— freedom in which to work
— an intellectual and verbal inheritance
— publication, contact

This is not an aside, because throughout Gould's essays we are reminded of the importance of "the rich tonal vocabulary of an inheritance". Gould has little to say directly about writing. He writes through analogy. His dissections of music and the recording phenomenon have a relationship with the structure and conveyance of written communication. Gould's passion was communication itself. His rejection of the concert stage revealed a need to, as they say, get into the music—what Gould called the "unsubstantial", "the disembodied" spirit of art, "the realm of technical transcendence"—and find a style that has "unity through intuitive perception, unity of craft and scrutiny, mellowed by mastery achieved..."

A sample of Gould's craft

In many respects, indeed, Schoenberg was the stuff of which Ken Russell screenplays are made. Despite a relatively quiet life on the domestic front (two wives, five children, several dogs, one rabbit), he gave full rein to an ego of Wagnerian proportions. In 1921, when he formulated the twelve-tone technique, he modestly declared that "I have ensured the supremacy of German music for the next hundred years." (Reviewer's note:

Would you believe thirty-five?) A compulsive teacher
and lawgiver, he became obsessed with the idea that
his students would endeavour to usurp his authority and pre-empt his innovatory claims. "Told Webern
about short pieces....Webern starts writing shorter and
shorter pieces—follows all my developments (exag-
gerates)....Webern seems to have used twelve tones
in some of his compositions *without telling me* [ital-
ics Schoenberg's]....Webern committed many acts of
infidelity with the intention of making himself the inno-
vator."

A sample of his wit

While alive, Webern was of interest only to colleagues;
his posthumous canonization was primarily an ac-
knowledgement of the ideas engendered by his work
and only secondarily attributable to the works per se.
(N.B. to G.G.: File under "Controversial Pronounce-
ments" and prepare defensive posture.) Hindemith, on
the other hand, always had a public—not, perhaps, the
sort of public that would turn up presold for the premiere
of a Shostakovitch symphony, no matter the rebuffs To-
varich Dmitri's last effort might have suffered via *Pravda*
and the Presidium, nor the sort that would attend at the
Royal Albert while Sir Adrian had a go at RVW's new
opus, secure in the knowledge that even if the Fourth
did defy good breeding and voice leading as the acad-
emy decreed, the chap is one of us and, given that,
Nostalgia Waives the Rules. (N.B. to G.G.: File under
"Potential Puns" and prepare defensive posture.)

Not everything in the volume sparkles with sarcastic
splendour. The liner-notes from *The Goldberg Variations*
have a sober serenity, and the articles on Arnold Schoenberg are packed with acute analyses of that composer's

twelve-tone theory. We should pay particular attention to what Gould says about Schoenberg, because he is an artist that Gould, in his ideas and his sense of mission, often identified himself with. (Note: Gould makes reference to the impact Thomas Mann's *Dr. Faustus* had on Schoenberg.)

All Gould's writings are caught in a squeeze between the scholastic and the journalistic. He had no intention of speaking only to specialists, scholars, and classical purists—the Protection Groups of the post-literate society. He wanted to reach the individual reader. But how do you grab hold of a readership when there is no longer a common literary ground? Gould held on to the hope that he could speak directly to the right receiver. It was this hope that drove conventional thinkers in art-music to dismiss him as a pop star; while, in the meantime, the pop audience continued to consider him (if at all) as a highbrow.

His pieces explore the potential of using rhetoric like a musician. The model of John Cage's remarkable book *Silence* is behind some of these essays. To achieve oral effects, Gould employs quotations, jokes, puns, dashes, brackets, alternating short sentences with long ones, using preludes, section edits, italics, ellipses, commas, and periods (to mark the rests and stops), abrupt paragraph breaks, and—a favourite device—the detailed list.

He puts the pun into punctuation.

In *Conversations*, Part I, he improvises seven variations on his keynote "tactile" (touch). He states "tactilia"; expands "tactile image"; elaborates "tactile configurations"; bridges to "tactile assumptions"; pauses on "tactile problems"; ponders "extra-tactile experience"; resolves with (half chord) "tactile compromise". The word focused on obsessively here is not repeated again in the book.

Gould obeys the technique of satire and adopts other narrative personae. He dons a new mask and criticizes his own excess. "I am fascinated with the fact that most of our value judgements relate to an awareness of identity," he comments in *Conversations*. Flexibility is the constant in his prose: he is willing to be absurd. At his worst he overwrites: his prose can be turgid, daunting, like some grotesque parody of a German academic. (Serenus Zeitblom in *Dr. Faustus*?) But agreement with his often rash opinions is not the point. Turn to any page of the *Reader* and you'll find him jazzing up his diction and syntax, to make his style individualized, to make us involved, his voice growing stronger and stranger, the titles reverberating with idiosyncrasy: "We Who Are about to Be Disqualified Salute You!" Not only "Make It New", but Make It Move.

> The great thing about the music of Richard Strauss is that it presents and substantiates *an argument which transcends all the dogmatisms of art*—all questions of style and taste and idiom—all the frivolous, effete preoccupations of the chronologist. It presents to us an example of the man who makes richer his own time by not being of it; who speaks for all generations by being of none. *It is the ultimate argument of individuality*—an argument that man can create his own synthesis of time without being bound by the conformities that time imposes. (My emphasis)

Yet behind Gould's mask of the solitary there is that *desperado* need for an astonishing union between projector and receiver, "an amalgam of ecstasy and reason". He was fleeing ordinary touch to find something sounder; he was charging the airwaves with his magnetic messages and verbal variations, asking: is anyone, anywhere, actually there?

Did he find that charged contact?

4

SPIRIT ON THE AIR

Behind Gould's desire to impart and inform is his belief that electronic circuitry steps up spiritualism and ethics. If the city is sometimes called second nature, then electric communication, Gould suggests, creates what we could call a supernature. This is the omnipresence of voice and image we find in Magnetic Cities through radios, TVs, computers, and telephones: it is a spiritism of sexual fantasies and *doppelgänger*, repeats and echoes, call-ups and key-ins. Gould remade himself into a vanishing artist at his listening post. He wanted to be a medium and use the spirit of recording to transmit his messages. Through his writings, Gould revealed himself ("analysis and dissection") to us. The ethical act: reconstructing

an awareness of identity

In his reviews and interviews, he hinted at patterns and plans that charted a way through a maze of thinking.
Watch when we begin to follow his clues.

Gould refers to George Santayana's *The Last Puritan* (1936), a novel about self-education. "I," Gould said, "perhaps rather than the hero of George Santayana's famous novel, am 'the Last Puritan'." In Santayana's *Memoir in the Form of a Novel*, two friends debate their eccentric acquaintance Oliver, who is the subject of the book.

"Had he a life to be written with a big L? And why should I, of all people, abandon philosophy in my old age and take to composing history, even supposing that in Oliver's history there were any actions to record?"

"No actions, but something you might take a wicked pleasure in describing: *Puritanism Self-Condemned. Oliver was The Last Puritan.*"

"I am afraid," I answered with a melancholy which was only half feigned, "I am afraid there will always be puritans in this mad world. *Puritanism is a natural reaction against nature.*" (My emphasis)

Here are more clues.

Gould's interest in Schoenberg and Thomas Mann has been remarked on. But Adrian Leverkühn, Mann's possessed composer in *Dr. Faustus* (English translation: 1949), attracted Gould with a strange intensity. Leverkühn is a composer who lives in shuttered rooms, uneasy in the light, carrying on debates between ego and superego (Self-Interviews), a musician who reinvents art out of parody and exhaustion. *Dr. Faustus* is narrated and reconstructed by Serenus Zeitblom, a musician-biographer who does not understand his friend's obsessions. (Like the author of *Glenn Gould: Music and Mind*?)

Leverkühn is reading Kierkegaard's essay on Mozart's "Don Juan" in *Either/Or*, when the devil appears. A contract is forged: "namely that the end belongs to us." Leverkühn's attempt to rediscover primeval inspiration is no longer a human one. It is a contract with the unseen.

At the same time that he retrieves creativity, Adrian suffers excruciating breakdowns; he withdraws from society; there is a hint that he is syphilitic, like Hugh Wolf and Nietzsche. He tries and fails to love a child named Echo (the Echo to his Narcissus); he destroys all human touch.

Mann intends a clear analogy to Nietzsche's life: the more isolated Leverkühn becomes, the more dehumanized his fantasies. Leverkühn composes new work, filling his space with tortured and technically demanding music, completing a final opus that ends in silence—like Mahler's Ninth Symphony, nicknamed "The Death Symphony"—and that will be his message of farewell, his hope that life will begin again.

Gould says

> ...this puritan view of the artist as a jeopardized being is not only dramatically viable but psychologically accurate. *It is the stuff of Faustus, to be sure, but it is the substance of lesser bargains as well.*...This view of the artist as wielder of demonic power, as a being whom ordinary beings should approach with caution, implicitly conveys a respect for his role. (My emphasis)

What did he mean by this track?

Investigate spiritism further.

We know Gould conducted most transactions on the telephone. Cott's *Conversations* adapts an interview held over three days. The interviewer admits that "during those phone conversations...Gould and I became friends...the phone made it easier for the pianist...." Existence was concentrated into interplays of static, disembodied voices, long-distance connections, "speech without walls". There is no telephonese, like computerese, to describe this aerial phenomenon. Yet Gould made the phone a central instrument in his repertoire of performing devices. "I separate myself from conflicting and contrasting notions," he said. The telephone offered him sanctuary and entrance. He could spring into his listener's ear using German, French, or Russian accents. For some users the phone can be a weapon, a license to obtrude. The telephone encourages monologue, the hotline, and masturbation. I've said that the power of Gould's writing comes from his off-balancing technique: we are continually put off guard. If we review Gould's long answers in Cott's book, then we realize that his telephone use is a link to his juggling of personae. Each time he called up it was as if he were trying out new identities that were like voices in a vast fugue he was composing in his mind, or searching for a fresh voice that would be as precise and shaped as an edited tape. These overtures spell out a technological guessing game

Who am I now?

Look for more clues to this private man whose every public utterance was news.

"The isle is full of noises, sounds, and sweet airs that give delight and hurt not," Shakespeare's Caliban says in *The Tempest*. While I write this in Toronto the Good, outside my window I can hear voices, cat cries, hydro wires, car horns and tires, a sonic battery not always registered but certainly felt. The city's sound track stamps your mind with repetition and conception. The delicate human tuning instrument vibrates to pressures we cannot see. If the body is a balanced receiving set, if we are pulling in signals meant for televisions, telephones, radios, and computers, is burnout one of the effects?

Place a satellite dish in a backyard. Switched on, stations materialize on a screen. Suppose you pick up the signals. Recall the phenomenon of hearing a favourite song running through your mind, then turning on a radio to find that same song playing. Suppose the body absorbs what the dishes catch. Suppose more: we talk of tension headaches and stress as if our own receptivity could be a trap.

Acid rain. Acid air. Chronic stress, migraines, trauma, sore corneas, bad nerves, paralysis, and blunting. "…pesticides are invisible, food additives are invisible, radioactivity is invisible," Jerome Deshusses writes in *The Eighth Night of Creation, Life on the Edge of Human History* (English translation: 1982).

> Even the most harmful automobile exhausts, such as carbon monoxide, are…inodorous, while lead, benzopyrene, and methylcholanthrene can be detected only with difficulty.…Accidents in nuclear power stations can affect public opinion…but their emissions are nothing in comparison with the kilos of plutonium that power stations release *imperceptibly* despite any system of purification.…

Hatred of your flesh, the desire to escape your own skin, feeling "out of touch", dispossessed, "beside yourself"—all this may be part of the sensation of saturation. Reaching out to others becomes a possible source of transmittable disease. So avoid the nudge, the grasp: they are the human contagion; get rid of the body, the feel of the world. But speaking out depends on a trust in others. Implicit faith: that the words will be admitted and remembered, that things change in the humanist transfer. Yet why add to verbal congestion? Why participate in "competitive frenzy"? Who can say that the word won't be polluted?

Why not avoid the urge to speak to others? Why not choose privacy? and purity?

In touch/out of touch...

In synch/out of synch...

These clichés preserve a truth about us. The human system requires a means of managing the information overload. Yet how can we preserve a private identity in the excess of input, the barrage of intrusions, the infiltrations of sound tracks, telephone buzzes, and verbal requests for access?

Now Toronto is known as the Clean City. It is a place that wants to be a magnetic centre, a financial capital, for North American waves. In this Dream City (the City of Trees), Gould and McLuhan speculated that we would register the outcome of communication overload, the outage, here before anywhere else. Both used publicity to dramatize their findings. But one sought purity, a celibate refinement of technique. Gould's filtering was done to convey ideas to those in need of imaginative links to a nature they did not perceive. He was an acoustic messenger, a carrier of a greater musical theme (harmony: "a joining together"), the *Gesamtkunstwerk,* the Wagnerian total form, art and instruments in a transformed aesthetic.

Gould held out a promise of revitalized play. On television, he was a tour guide for CBC cameras: he ushered viewers around "the North American suburban dream", a "truly peaceful" environ, an idealized object to be studied as if under glass—or from inside a car— a place of orderly dreams (Peter Ustinov: "New York as if run by the Swiss"), a city in search of a name in the teleglobe, where movie producers import garbage to make the streets look dirty. Gould chose Toronto because he could tune out and, when he wished, tune in to be the escort to technological awe.

We have observed how sensitive Gould was to turns in the weather and to room temperature. So to insulate himself he dressed up like an intellectual from Dostoevski's *The Possessed*. "Fragile....Breakable Material Inside." The cost of shut-out can be shut down. To rectify the imbalance you put out information. And Gould talked. And clowned. Out poured his reviews, interviews, and disc-cussions. Gould wore what Canetti would term his acoustic mask: he was a zealous advocate of contrary views. Though Gould despised polemics, he nevertheless was a masterful polemicist. His conversation was extended by digressions and occasional avoidance of direct answers: "Ask me that again in a year," he would say; when he paused, he let his "um" sound like a stand-in for "om". He seemed to be vanishing, disappearing, resisting....Listen to me, but leave me alone, he suggested; "I vibrate, therefore I am," he quipped.

I have remarked that electronic communications create feelings of omnipresence: the God complex. Yet even in a specially constructed silent chamber, John Cage said, the music you hear will be your own. Heartbeats, blood pulse, and breathing. There is, in short, no escape from rhythm and receptivity. You can of course try: the history of our time is a record of the attempt to amputate sensitivity from the self. The hunger for making yourself impervious, for depersonalizing, and for turning others into inhumans (vermin), machines, or superhumans (gods), may take many forms. William Butler Yeats, in later years, in the unpublished "Seven Propositions" stated that the physical world was provisional and insubstantial, and that the spirit world was true existence. Yeats couldn't count out cock and cunt, though he made various tries. The electric media's creation of a supernature found premonitions in artists who sought a definition of modern life. Gould explored the spiritual potency of recording and channelled his sexuality into machines. Norman Mailer, "a psychic outlaw", built his *oeuvre* out of the need to feel flesh. *Ancient Evenings* (1983) commences with a citation from Yeats's *Ideas of Good and Evil*. And in Mailer's misunderstood prose poem, he made our time parallel with the ancient Egyptians and their doctrine of floating souls yearning for the rite inhabitation, an entry into a new body. Like J. G. Ballard's visionary stories, or the film *Blade Runner*, the images in *Ancient Evenings* lead to the discarnate. Mailer's first sentences: "Crude thoughts and fierce forces are my state. I do not know who I am. Nor what I was....Is one Human? Or merely alive?" His last: "We sail across dominions barely seen, washed by the swells of time. We plow through fields of magnetism. Past and future come together on thunderheads and our dead hearts live with lightning in the wounds of Gods." Plunge into the abyss of the spirit of the thing, and the metaphors turn towards reincarnation, ghosts, and gods.

The threads between these artists?

Matters of identity: inspired or dis-spirited individuals, phantasmic and drifting, integrity shredded, turning towards either bestiality or incarnations of hope.

Washroom graffiti
**WHEN YOU ARE ON
THE RADIO
YOU ARE
THE STATION**

Well, it's right to be skeptical about all this. The subjects are massive, and abstract. I can only touch on them. And the deeper we search for a reel Gould, the deeper we go into science fiction.

Still, we question what cryptic keys Gould sensed in the intervals between his music and writings, why he pondered private identity, using pseudonyms like Dr. Herbert von Hochmeister, cruising incognito in the north ("I am a motel man myself"), flipping stations on the radio band, practising on his piano with a vacuum cleaner humming, experiencing perpetual playback, teasing his readers with his preference for Petula Clark over the Beatles, and then declaring that his favourite "Pet" Clark songs were "Downtown" and "Who Am I?"

"I cannot bear assaults of any kind," he said to Jonathan Cott.

The more he became like a Robinson Crusoe inspecting studio tracks, the more inescapable he seemed. Those who had never met him accounted for his presence by dropping a needle on a record's edge and gazing at the familiar figure on the jacket sleeve.

One Sunday afternoon while writing this essay, I switched the radio on to the CBC-FM. And there was Gould's voice, quick, now, here, proselytizing on the art of the studio. That was his key. He was our Glenn Gould, a New Player recreated out of "the privacy and ecstasy", and potential "life" after death, recordings could bring.

"We have begun to think musically," Victor Zuckerkandl proclaims in *Sound and Symbol: Music and the External World* (English translation: 1956), "when, then, music becomes the *key* that leads to a new understanding of the world of the psyche, or organisms, even of inorganic matter, what is taking place here if not a comprehensive *musicalization* of thought, a change that seems to be opening new roads to our understanding and, indeed, to our logic?"

Jimi Hendrix on the radio years ago

> Like it's electric-city....I feel it every time I plug in....And someday...it'll take me all the way there...the electric church....Pure mind...

Gould believed that society was altering its sense ratio. Voyeurism and unlimited creation. Amputation and humanism. Post-literacy and a new listener. Muzak and a library of classics. Surveillance and communion. Selfishness and selflessness. Invasion and vulnerability. We are in the unknown, reeling in outages of seduction and nausea, resistance and saturation, commitment and passivity, unable to see whether our pact with electric supernature is benign or malignant—an educating creation or a race that could kill—an ambiguous state in which all the old moral values, the black-and-white distinctions, may no longer apply.

5

SILENCE

I return to my uneasiness when I consider *The Glenn Gould Reader* and the *Conversations*. The turbulence in Gould's prose style, the convulsions of manner, suggest a man locked into a struggle with something that is never identified. A rage for order storms on in those pages. Gould repeatedly refers to a desire for tranquillity. His rejection of the concert stage was determined because, he claimed, he disliked "temptation", "exhibitionism", and "worldly hedonism", and wished to achieve "ecstatic contemplation". However, the effect of his style is anything but tranquil. The writing is on the contrary full of forward movement. There are occasions in the *Reader* when Gould's avowed intention fiercely collides with the literary impact.

His style is sometimes at odds with the content.

The thick layers of eighteenth-century-style prose, with its extended paragraphs and digressions, seem wilful in the attempt to arrest the writer's own push. It is as if in the latter part of his life he longed for something he couldn't achieve. But what?...peace? When I recalled the last performance of *The Goldberg Variations*, with its personalized and exaggerated dynamics and tempi, the unreleased version of Wagner's *Siegfried Idyll* conducted at a glacial pace by Gould, his declaration that he was giving up the piano for composing and conducting, the picture of him for the cover of *The Goldberg Variations* looking hunched, ghostly, balding, a burned-out substitute for the once dashing performer—I began to wonder what psychological state he was in towards the end of his life.

The wondering is fuelled by the fact that the *Reader* is arranged thematically and not chronologically. Dates are provided at the bottom of the page, so you can do detective work. I found those essays written in the 1970s at the height of his reclusiveness more stylistically reckless than the pieces written in the 1950s and '60s. If the *Reader* had been arranged chronologically, we would have been exposed to an explicit autobiographical record. The effect of this would have been intriguing and, finally, saddening. For Gould's later essays seem driven by his desire to transcend humanness, to escape time, the judgement of history, what he calls "mere chronology".

Gould spent his life mixing European and North American co-ordinates of culture. He tried to be an Aerial without restrictions of body, time, and place. Typically, when he refers to Canada, it is his ground, mere space. "The Idea of North" was for Gould an emptiness waiting for re-creation: the North was a landscape of leaves, wind, water, elements to be managed by his (limitless?) electronic imagination. And in the last version of *The Goldberg Variations* you hear in the Aria a concern for the space between the notes as you never have before.

Rest, arrest.

Enigmatically, the Last Puritan seemed to look for one more transforming break, "building into art a component that will enable it to preside over its own obsolescence".

He was searching for something beyond art, and perhaps his instruments, trying to make "paradise/*terrestre*".

The pure note; the pure conductor. Gould was pursued by a "primeval curiosity which seeks to uncover in the relations of statement and answer...of challenge and response, of call and of echo the secret of those still, desert places, which hold the clues to man's destiny."

With his telephone arias and elaborate masks, his isolation and insistence on the sanctity of the studio, it was as if Glenn Gould personally aspired to a condition of music. But he could not stop what was obsessing or possessing him into an early grave. He said, "I should like to spend an entire winter in the dark." And at the end of his search for the right note and the purified space, he had turned full circle, back to the Bach *Variations* with which he had begun. Beyond that, there was no call, no response; only the clichés, the noise, and the interference of those who could not comprehend his receptivity.

Thus the last possible rest was—and had to be— silence.

APPREHENSIONS NOW: CANETTI AND McLUHAN

1

Apprehend: to lay hold of, to fear. In Latin, the root *"prehendere"* means "to seize". A distant echo: to grasp, as if by hand. *"Carpe diem"*: a translation, not simply "live for the day", but *Seize the Day*, the name of one of Saul Bellow's best books, a novella about apprehending sudden truth. And "now"? "Modern" comes from the Latin *"modo"* meaning "just now". Apprehension is perception under pressure. Apprehensions Now is the attempt to grasp hold of the world, our words, and what may be passing.

Elias Canetti and Marshall McLuhan.

They may seem like an impossible pairing. Canetti is an essayist-novelist from a Jewish European background, an intellectual who emerged from the revolutionary milieu of the 1920s and '30s, the decades of Freud and Lenin and the rise of National Socialism in Germany. He is the author of a novel, plays, prose poems, essays, a book of aphorisms, three volumes of an as-yet-uncompleted autobiography, and the seminal *Crowds and Power.* Marshall

McLuhan was a teacher, a philosopher, a satirist, certainly something of a poet, a Catholic convert who lived most of his life in Canada. McLuhan was for a time in the 1960s a media celebrity. However, no one talks of McLuhanism and McLuhanites these days. Canetti has taken the route of silence, exile, and cunning: there are not, and there never have been, any "Canetti-ism" or "Canetti-ites". McLuhan admired Canetti, and though there is no record of Canetti's opinion of McLuhan, their visions coincide and collide. Both are concerned with present configurations of power, mass society, language, and change. Both considered what to do with the literate power at their command: how to find an audience. "Literature as a profession is destructive," Canetti says; "one should fear words more." Configurations are prefigurations. What was it they were trying to send out to us, and to apprehend?

The convergence between the two thinkers begins with Canetti's only novel, *Auto-da-Fé* (German: 1935; English: 1946) and extends to McLuhan's *The Gutenberg Galaxy: The Making of Typographic Man* (1962). The original German title of Canetti's novel is *Die Blendung*, or *The Blinding*. Neither *Auto-da-Fé* nor *The Tower of Babel*, as the novel is sometimes called, indicates the meaning of the German words. I have no idea why these other titles were used and, frankly, C.V. Wedgwood's translation is inadequate to the original German. The novel is *The Blinding*: these words preserve the intended pun on insight and the loss of the individual "I". In all my readings of McLuhan, I haven't found a single reference to Canetti's grim, fascinating work; and yet nearly twenty-seven years before the publication of *The Gutenberg Galaxy*, Canetti was warning us about the close of the book age.

2

On the street. A bookstore declares

CLEARANCE SALE

"Books!" a customer says, "Well, who has the time? It's either read or make money. Well, I read to put myself to sleep you see. I mean—look! I've cancelled my subscription to *Time* magazine. So...books. No. But I do love them, yes. They're still my favourites. I just love to stop in front of bookstores...."

Now: Canetti's story in *The Blinding* is simple. A renowned Sinologist, Peter Kien, is abruptly catapulted through a series of strange circumstances into a bizarre reality. Kien is a university professor, a man of strict punctuality and self-discipline, a man who thinks in systems and theories. We first glimpse him during his morning walk around his city, a habit to which he obsessively adheres, like Immanuel Kant in Königsberg.

Scene: Kien engages a boy in talk in front of a book-store window. A mock Socratic dialogue ensues. The boy is tested as if he is a student in a catechism held out of doors. Kien asks examination questions.

"Can you read?"

"Which would you prefer, a piece of chocolate or a book?"

"Would you like to travel to a foreign country?"

"You must have read a great deal already."

"Who wrote this book? Can you remember?"

The examiner discovers that "his student" is intrigued by Kien's own specialty, Chinese characters. The boy passes Kien's test. "You should come and see my library one day." Then Canetti describes Kien, "by nature morose", chastizing himself for indulging in conversation. The teacher without a classroom retreats into the silence of his study.

Kien "preferred to express himself in the written rather than the spoken word". He is a print man who lives alone; he avoids public gatherings and does not like to be touched by other people. Kien no longer has to show up anywhere to prove a point to his colleagues. His reputation and name carry sufficient weight.

Later Kien is tricked out of his library by his former housekeeper and new wife, Theresa, who, incidentally, cannot read. He is thrown from privacy into a public underworld populated by a "manic, exuberant" dwarf named Fischerle, and by beggars and criminals. Driven mad by his sinister experiences, Kien is placed under the eye of his psychiatrist brother, Georges.

Georges is a shadow image of the reclusive Peter, a repressive power man, a psychoanalyst who finds pleasure in controlling his neurotic patients. His obsession is "the effects of the mass on history...and in the life of individuals...Countless people go mad because the mass in them is...strongly developed." All members of a crowd are equal: they follow a senseless rhythm. Dr. Kien wants to level everyone to an unimaginative unity; people are then easy to place. Georges misinterprets Kien's malaise (a foreshadowing of Canetti's rejection of Freudianism), and confines the scholar to a bed in his library. There Kien has his suicidal breakdown.

The novel ends in a holocaust of books.

> The books cascade off the shelves on to the floor. He takes them up in his long arms. Very quietly, so that they can't hear him outside, he carries pile after pile into the hall....And while the frantic din tears his brain to fragments, he builds a mighty bulwark out of books. The hall is filled with volume upon volume....He places the ladder in the middle of the room where it stood before. He climbs up to the sixth step, looks down on the fire and waits....When the flames reached him at last, he laughed out loud, louder than he had ever laughed in all his life.

The burning is Kien's defiance, his revolt against his jailers. But the result is that all his books have been fed into a furnace.

Kien is the literary person isolated in a universe of notes, cross-references, and quotes. He lives half of a Cartesian mind-body split. He is all brain. The three parts of *The Blinding* are titled: "A head without a world", "Headless world", and "The world in the head". These reveal the narrative progression, though the novel is not as schematic as I may be making it sound.

Peter Kien, the man of systems and theories, is a thinker without a moral imagination. He is the solitary writer living in abstraction: the Book Man as Bookworm. When Kien suffers his collapse, it is because the brute facts of reality have devastated him. And yet when Kien is confronted by events in the streets, the novel turns grotesque, hyper-real; the images become brutal, the street-scenes like Expressionist set-pieces from Fritz Lang's *M*. And the last pages, with Kien's library crackling into a furnace, seem like a prophecy....But a prophecy of what? The impotence of the literary person? the dying tradition of books? both the destruction of words and the destructive potential in language itself?

Years after the publication of *The Blinding*, Thomas Mann (who had read Canetti's novel) was warned by friends, while he was on a speaking tour in Switzerland, not to return to Germany. The Nazis were setting his books to the torch. Canetti's second volume of memoirs, which describes the genesis of *The Blinding*, is called *The Torch in my Ear* (German: 1980; English: 1982). Canetti went into exile in France and England, fleeing the war and the hounding of the Jews. The torch in the book's title is taken from the name of Karl Kraus's notorious satirical magazine of the 1920s and '30s, *Die Fackel—The Torch*. Kraus was the satirist-scourge of Vienna, a polemicist whose "voice of destruction" and authority stirred the young Canetti. Kraus's torch is the fire of illumination and the fire of opposition to his age. Thus two fires burn in Canetti's imagination—memory and words: the blaze of destruction and the blaze of illumination. *The Blinding* describes the flash of paradoxical insight: the moment when the "I" is blinded by what it sees. McLuhan himself notes: "The ancient seer was typically figured as blind. He lived by insight."

Canetti's insight is that the fires of annihilation and revelation are often the same: they are born out of each other. This is why it is difficult for us to tell who is dedicated to dialogue and who to propaganda (coercive monologue). Or: why it is hard for us to see who is devoted to enlightenment and who to blitzkrieg.

The secluded scholar unprepared for confusion and chaos is savagely satirized in *The Blinding*. In this satire, Canetti may also be smashing and scrutinizing himself; for he too was a bookish student, fascinated by Sinology, stunned by a riot in Vienna on July 15, 1927, when the Palace of Justice was burned down. Canetti's first drafts of *The Blinding* refer to Kien as the Book Man, and Kant, and Brand. From the start, however, the Book Man is a passive, hypnotized creature. Kien himself is one in the line of Faustian figures walled up inside their libraries as if locked in a mausoleum, a museum, or a zoo. In the early stages, the manuscript was called *Brand Catches Fire*, and then *Kant Catches Fire*. The novel was intended as the first in a long series, *The Human Comedy of Madmen*, a modernist updating of Dante's *Inferno,* a diabolical retuning of Balzac. Canetti never completed these works, and instead turned to his research into the crowd. All that remains of *The Human Comedy* is *Ear-Witness* (German: 1974; English: 1979), a book of fragments, of sketches with titles like "The Name Licker" and "The Marrow-smeller". In its published form, *The Blinding* is a prophetic witnessing, filled with foreboding about death, sex—another fire—and the obliteration of individual identity.

(Note: Umberto Eco's *The Name of the Rose* echoes the situation of the guardian intellectual in the library and climaxes with the burning of books and manuscripts and the scattering of leaves over a Europe in ruins. It can be read as a post-literate parable—in the guise of a medieval whodunit—of the University as Holy Church, with the scholar as monk, the critic as Holmesian investigator.)

The Blinding may also be a metaphoric prefiguring of *The Gutenberg Galaxy: The Making of Typographic Man* and McLuhan's probe into the transition between literate awareness and the electronic age.

> What will be the new configurations of mechanisms and of literacy....Even without collision, such co-existence of technologies and awareness brings tension and trauma to every living person. Our most ordinary and conventional attitudes seem suddenly twisted into gargoyles and grotesques. Familiar institutions and associations seem at times menacing and malignant. (*The Gutenberg Galaxy*)

3

Then a memory that haunts: Marshall McLuhan sitting at the long table in the darkened Centre for Culture and Technology. Silent. Evening. His speech paralysed. McLuhan has to be read to. In front of him on the table is the manuscript of *The Laws of the Media*, uncompleted, in fragments. The unpublished manuscript was to be the culmination of his life work; it would offer the perceptual method that he had exhausted his life searching for.

McLuhan nods as details of the manuscript are explained. Page by page. Then: stop.

He lost his speech gradually. It took two days after the first stroke. Words then had to be retrieved and reshaped. It was as if people had to find a new language to communicate with him. All you could do was gesture, and talk.

The University of Toronto shut down his Centre; and the universities largely continue to ignore his thinking. McLuhan was once omnipresent in discussions about technology, literacy, and the global village; he now stands in the solitude of a reputation that is nowhere.

Something else that haunts me: people travelling at the speed of light. The self is dissolved like a note in an accelerating run of music. Musicalized being. The monotype becomes the stereotype when everyone is moving too much or too fast to touch or remember.

Relevant glosses from *The Gutenberg Galaxy*

Does the interiorization of media such as "letters" alter the ratio among the senses and change mental processes?

The print-made split between head and heart is the trauma which affects Europe from Machiavelli till the present.

The portability of the book, like that of the easel-painting, added much to the new cult of individualism.

The twentieth century encounter between alphabetic and electronic faces of culture confers on the printed word a crucial role in staying the return to "the Africa within".

"The Africa within" is the heart of darkness. This is, McLuhan knew, a central metaphor in the modern journey to the dark side of human nature. *The Blinding* itself echoes *Samson Agonistes* and the scream of blindness ("Oh, dark, dark, dark"), and also resembles Kurtz's "the horror, the horror".

While McLuhan's perceptions and intuitions are urgent, they were not tragic in their implications. His response was to turn to public alert through satire and laughter: the exposure of the power of all media, electric and literary.

McLuhan's and Canetti's perception of the end of the Book Age, or of the transformation and displacement of the Book Man, signals what followed in their complex thinking processes. McLuhan may have experienced some sort of blinding; he worked with flashes of intuition; however, I've never found a reference to an event that inspired the illumination. There may not have been one event: rather, a series of successive re-cognitions. Still, after decades in print, *The Gutenberg Galaxy* remains a daring, unsettling book. Fact: McLuhan and Canetti continued their intuitions with attempts to illuminate the irrational mass movements of the century.

After *The Blinding*, Canetti abandoned the novel form. He devoted himself for more than fifteen years to the researching and writing of his non-fiction magnum opus, *Crowds and Power* (German: 1960; English: 1962). Again the German title carries more motion: *Masse und Macht.*

For *Crowds and Power*, Canetti became an expert on forms of coercion, on the disintegration of a centred self into a centreless mass. He recognizes that the crowd will be the ground for the individual. How do you make your way through a crowd? Study its habits; go into the environment and make notes; record the context of the private self. *Crowds and Power* is an inventory of grotesques, a vision of "crystals", "hunting packs", and "rings"; it is punctuated by the "laments" and "howls" of the hunter and the hunted. Canetti examines the hypnotic spell of the deranged leader who slaughters others for being merely persons. He fears the crowd impulse. Frenzy and passivity are his twin villains. Though Hitler, Stalin, and other mass killers are not mentioned in the work, the Schreber case in the chapter "Rulers and Paranoics" is used as a metaphor for all overlords. Schreber is the dictator in microcosm; he is the paranoid ordering his opponents to oblivion from an isolated cell. Schreber treats the outer world as an abstraction, and he wants to kill it. Ominously, Schreber resembles Kien in *The Blinding*, the intellectual locked up in his solipsistic jail, like a Céline conjuring imaginary carnage, vengeance, and punishment.

Throughout *Crowds and Power*, Canetti attempts to appeal to the Plain Reader as if conversing with us outside the claims of government, corporation, university, or lobby group. A crowd will always show the intelligence of its least intelligent member. Tyrants turn their subjects into undifferentiated mass. Rob a tyranny of the sting of command, and the Plain Citizen cannot be coerced into corporate service. For Canetti, every case is unique: we are all exceptions. True communication, he suggests, takes place between individuals.

The fear in *Crowds and Power* comes from someone who was a witness to mass hysteria in Europe during World War II. That fear of the mob disturbs populist democrats who see in the emotion a nostalgia for absolutes or a secret yearning for dictatorship. This is not Canetti's point. Without the ability to stand apart and read patterns in history, we are open to being channelled into destruction.

However, any attack on the mass is a deconsecrating act. So *Crowds and Power* is a challenge to read. When Canetti studied crowd formations, he explored actual physical movements. This makes the book intensely metaphoric. Sociologists dislike the method. They call it poetry. *Crowds and Power* is authentically poetic: it asks the reader to see, think, feel, hear, and touch, in a sensuous apprehension. It uses art and intuition as a way of knowing. Compare Erich Fromm's *The Anatomy of Human Destructiveness* (1973) with *Crowds and Power,* and note the sharp

contrast between a fine moralist-philosopher and a novelist grasping hold of reality. Mind, tension, clarity, passion,
and liberty are Canetti's responsibilities.

A sample of his dramatizing technique

> Man has always listened to the footsteps of other men;
> he has certainly paid more attention to them than to
> his own. Animals too have their familiar gait; their
> rhythms are often richer and more audible than those
> of men; hoofed animals flee in herds, like regiments of
> drummers. The knowledge of the animals by which he
> was surrounded, which threatened him and which he
> hunted, was man's oldest knowledge.

Crowds and Power reads like an imagistic sequel
to *The Blinding:* the essay as novel. There are times
when it seems more autobiographical and confessional
than his third volume of memoirs, *The Play of the Eyes*
(1986). Throughout *Crowds and Power*, there are unstated
personal confrontations: Canetti *vs.* the Nietzscheans (the
superman "bullies"), Canetti *vs.* Marxism (history as class
struggle and revolution), Canetti *vs.* the Freudians (the
sexual reductionists). By blasting out these philosophical
bases, he suspends every reader over an abyss of decision.
Burn the books in your mind. See things fresh. Then ask:
what is valuable? how do we get at the true?

To seize the day, Canetti works by aphorism, image,
paradox, parody, quotation. He does not take the route of
his mad Book Man and write an academic treatise. The
aphorism is an arresting guide: it allows the reader to
breathe between the lines.

> The moment of survival is the moment of power.

> A Buddha today—unthinkable, even a Christ. All that's
> possible is a Mohammed.

> Travelling, one accepts everything; indignation stays
> at home. One looks, one listens, one is roused to
> enthusiasm by the most dreadful things because they
> are new. Good travellers are heartless.

> After the destruction, crowd and fire die away.

Canetti and McLuhan radically diverge in the intensity of their moral visions. Canetti has not shown an interest in reading the images of pop culture, the North American ground. He is in the central-European intellectual tradition of Hermann Broch, Robert Musil, and Karl Kraus. Canetti perceives the collapse of literacy and perspective in tragic-absurd terms: he is catastrophe-haunted. He has described his writing process as resembling a running for cover in a bomb raid. He has lived a displaced life: Vienna, Paris, Berlin, London; he is, like George Steiner, unhoused and polyglot, a citizen of the world who has not capitulated to despair. He called his first volume of memoirs *The Tongue Set Free* (German: 1977; English: 1979). The suggestion: you have to cross borders, transcend national boundaries, to locate the human province.

Canetti's urgency, however, is hounded by ghosts of viciousness and violence.

> Even after the first war, some writers were still able
> to content themselves with deep breathing and crystal
> polishing. But today, after the second war, after gas
> chambers and atomic bombs, being human requires
> more in its utmost imperilment and degradation. One
> must turn to brutality as it always was, and coarsen
> one's hands and mind on it. One must grab man as
> he is, hard and unredeemed. But one must not permit
> him to lay his hands on hope. Hope can flow only from
> darkest knowledge, otherwise it will become a derisive

superstition and speed up the destruction that looms more and more ominously. (*The Human Province*)

Marshall McLuhan was a North American intellectual involved in the contract with the New World. He extended the vision of Cosmic Man and the global village that Wyndham Lewis himself had first described. McLuhan is also in the tradition of Canadian thinkers and artists fascinated by communication signals and reception. He was realistic about any attempt to shut off electric input and influence: it was impossible. In the post-literate society, literacy could function as a DEW line: the Distant Early Warning about overload, saturation, and dissolution of individual integrity. Literacy kept you critically conscious: it could restore the balance to the imbalance of instantaneous information. The printed word could be a weapon against unconscious drift. The eighteenth-century focus on language, education, and debate could work like a still point in the electronic wave.

And *Après mot, le déluge*. McLuhan, like Lewis, believed you could laugh your enemies to death. His puns, put-ons, and probes were charged with cosmopolitan hilarity. "I would not," Lewis says in *Blasting and Bombardiering,* "have you think that I am shut out from what is called by the Japanese 'the Ah-ness of things'....But there is a *ho-ho-ness* too...to proceed with a protracted comedy, which glitters against the darkness." To outwit the forces of surveillance and death, let the critical "I" become a private eye.

McLuhan's wit was *self*-protective. "If any person became totally aware of what is going on today, he'd go instantly mad." And: "The young people of today undergo a psychic torture through media bombardment and fallout that is unprecedented." His approach is comic-apocalyptic, though we can see him as a chronicler of disintegration and reintegration. McLuhan constantly referred to Edgar Allan Poe's "The Descent into the Mael-strom" because it served him as a metaphor for the inner necessity of creating a calm "I" in the midst of terror and turbulence.

But he said: "I never gave my books the full attention they deserved." It has to be admitted that McLuhan's books after *Understanding Media: The Extensions of Man* (1964) do not carry the concentration of form and language that distinguishes a great writer. McLuhan's reliance on aphorism and public performance led him to lose that attention to the literary work itself. The incomplete state of his last manuscripts came in part from his seeking after collaboration. His emphasis was always on teaching and forum: contact with others. His ideas live in sparks. The verb form "understanding" implies process and self-education; the book is not called "Media Understood".

The Blinding and *Crowds and Power* bear the mark of a disciplined stylist who has confronted his traumatized psyche. *The Blinding* can be frenetic and terrifying: it has a rhetoric of devastation. *Crowds and Power* is written in the language of recovery: it is contained and solid, like a calm response to the fury unleashed in Canetti's own fiction. His style is lean, crystalline, and emphatic; it embodies a code of self-conscious reseeing. Like Kafka, Canetti is careful about how much he says. It is as if, after *The Blinding*, he committed himself to rethinking the phenomenon of violence itself. Thus Canetti's recurrent word in Ralph Manheim's translation of *The Play of the Eyes* is "merciless".

We know that McLuhan made use of Canetti's books in *From Cliché to Archetype* and *Culture Is Our Business*. Can we imagine Canetti reading McLuhan?

It is hard to imagine Canetti reading any of his North American contemporaries with pleasure. Canetti would have been appalled by McLuhan's lack of a sense of darkness, his temporary identification with the media forces that McLuhan himself privately criticized. Canetti's writings, however, are unobservant about electric force fields and masses: he seems unaware of the effect of hyper-speed, the hyper-society that interrupts and corrodes awareness. Some of *Crowds and Power* is only exact and beautiful description. He seems to be always preparing himself to write. The effect: a vague feeling of incompletion; a sense that *Crowds and Power* is a set of notes intended for an opus yet to be written.

Canetti's humourless humanism and rigorous skepticism do reject the technological *Übermensch*, the super-being beyond criticism and beyond physical reach, the being that wants to dominate and program its surroundings. Canetti rejects a strain of satire because he will not use letters to kill; he will not be part of a pack; he will defy those who force us into brutality; and he will side with the creature. He is not interested in overcoming human nature, making man a god, a hero, an angel. He has grasped that the problem of our time is, simply, the definition of the human contract.

"In the age of the organ transplant," McLuhan writes, "the definition of 'death' has become problematic." We are already superhuman through our on-line computers, amplifiers, home-video reproductions, our fantasy systems that can mesmerize and duplicate our imperfect selves. A crowd cannot speak out; it can only groan, cheer, or wave. But to speak in a singular voice, and treat others as real, becomes more and more difficult. It is their efforts for the maintance of a humanism in the vortex of mass society that unites Canetti and McLuhan.

4

A nightclub, after hours.

    "Fuck, man," a man said.

    "Yeah?" his partner said.

    "Ah y'know. Fuck this, fuck that, fuck me, fuck you."

    "Yeah, I know."

    "Yeah. And I got another fuckin' problem."

    "What's that?"

    "The only fuckin' thing I can say any more is fuck."

    "That's too bad."

    "Fuckin' right."

Now I'd like to speak personally about my own interest in being a writer today.

From *The Blinding* to *The Gutenberg Galaxy* we see how two classically trained literary men, universalist in their traditions, moved to describe the motions of power and influence, the word in time. McLuhan and Canetti followed lucid lines: Canetti, an indirect and solitary route; McLuhan, plunging into the media maelstrom, risking distortion, marshalling whatever channels he found open, from TV to *Playboy*. It has been said by others that the role of the author is obsolete, so I'll pursue McLuhan's perception that books have lost their position as cultural guides.

Voltaire could shake his age through words. We call the eighteenth century the Age of Voltaire and sometimes the Age of Rousseau. Voltaire was an adversarial force; "he taught our time how to think," an admirer said; he was "the last happy writer" for Roland Barthes. Gloss: the author had a recognized role to play in society.

In the twentieth century, Wyndham Lewis, Ezra Pound, and other modernists sought to turn the tide of their time with novels, poems, essays, pamphlets, and polemics. They too were regarded as dangerous. The title of the Lewis play in *Blast* is *The Enemy of the Stars;* he later trimmed that title, applied it to himself, and to a magazine, and emerged as The Enemy, the ogre of Bloomsbury. But Lewis and Pound suffered rejection. Lewis went into exile in Canada, where he met McLuhan. (Lewis dubbed Toronto "a sanctimonious icebox".) Pound gave frenzied radio monologues, then ended in the Pisan Cage, in political treason, in St. Elizabeth's Insane Asylum in Washington, D.C., then in silence in Venice.

For a period, they were like caged men, symbolically suffering in advance the displacement of the book.

McLuhan himself has too long been misinterpreted as anti-book. Now his true impact seems to be subterranean. He is the unacknowledged underground for many writers and thinkers. Canetti, however, sensed from the beginning that a consciously critical writer could defy from the margins, outside the centres of electric power. Do we not speak of the writer—if he isn't a media celebrity or doesn't resemble Al Pacino—as a marginal being?

The literate person is an outsider today. Yet this exile, as it were, may give the literate person an advantage.

To read and write may be as unique an accomplishment as it was in pre-literate societies, in the thirteenth century, the time of *The Name of the Rose*. Readers and writers will have the role of maintaining the freshness and ferocity of language. They will have the job of staying out of tune: to make certain that human beings remain complex. The post-literate state may tell us why those writers with nineteenth-century views of the Heroic Author sound like anachronisms. When an author exerts the same mass-public appeal on his time as a Romantic-Heroic author, then the relationship with the audience is based on a sentimental nostalgia. The word can too easily be dismissed.

Canetti has said that we cannot permit ourselves the luxury of a sentimental hope. Instant meltdown looms. What form can an eccentric literary influence take? To go beyond the wordlessness, the cynicism, and the shining surface of society, and recover the power of words. There is no way out from a critical confrontation with our world. We must probe at issues, ideas, and popular fronts; even at risk of losing a voice in the consuming-consumer rush; even at risk of having the questioning cheapened, forgotten, and flattered for the wrong reasons. Even in Canada, in the midst of post-literacy: my place, my here.

5

In *The Blinding*, Canetti satirizes Kien, the aloof Sinologist, the head without a world. His Book Man literally goes up in smoke. But Canetti did not discard books. He worked slowly, but there was no desertion. He says in *The Human Province* (German: 1973; English: 1978): "Excluding the world, so important from time to time, is permissible only if it floods back in with greater force." McLuhan never withdrew; he remained available. Even his aphasia has a metaphorical significance to his inquiries. He said in his characteristic way: "In the age of the information hunter, feedback yields to feedforward, the point of view becomes the probe. Problems become discoveries."

Is there a middle way between the isolated Book Man and the super-real star?

That's a question I can't truly answer.

Yet this crucial teacher and this impassioned author offer methods of communication in the post-literate society: indirect, but at a still point of working outwards. Canetti supplied a credo in 1955 for any writer

To the administrator of words, whoever he may be: Give me dark words and give me clear words, but I want no flowers, you can keep the fragrance for yourself. I want words that don't fall away, words that don't wither. I want thorns and roots, and occasionally, very occasionally, a translucent leaf...

In a novel, a library burns. Blackened books; crackling papers; dried leaves; ash smell. The Book Man is consumed on his pyre of books. "Fire," he shouts. The burning spreads faster and faster. But the writer imagines this annihilation, trains himself to find the words that push from solitude outwards, an old message reaching from author to reader, calling and repeating

Where are you? What is your stand? Can you respond?
Are you there?
Are you there?
Are you there?

ACKNOWLEDGEMENTS

Portions of *The Solitary Outlaw* (*TSO*) were presented in very different forms in *Canadian Forum*, *Blast 3*, *Books in Canada*, and at the International Seminar on Pop Culture in Toronto in 1984.

TSO was written with the inspiration and help of Eric McLuhan and Kenneth Sherman. E.M. discussed ideas; K.S. gave stimulus for imagery. My sincere thanks to both.

Special thanks to Pierre Elliott Trudeau for permission to quote from his selected writings.

My thanks to Peter Brown at Piaget for permission to quote from the Wyndham Lewis books published by Black Sparrow Press.

Thanks also to Stanley Colbert for his patience and faith. Also thanks to Shirley Brimacombe for her typing wizardry and editorial acumen.

Others have contributed, suggested, debated, and criticized: B.A.P., A.M.P., Kats, and JUT; Frauke Voss (the soul in the fibre); Louise Oborne (who first heard it and said it was okay); T.C. McLuhan; Malcolm Lester;

Louise Dennys; Matthew Corrigan; William Aide; Barry Callaghan; Irving Layton; Senator Keith Davey; Fraser Sutherland; Joe Keogh (one of the unacknowledged legislators); David McKee; Ted Plantos; David Warren; Mrs. G.K. Brady; the Roberts clan; Thadaney Wittermann Design Communications; Roger Davies and everyone at MDC; the Ontario Arts Council; R.A. Paskauskas; Margaret Woollard, Tara McMurtry, all at Lester & Orpen Dennys; and, of course, as always, G.S.

My special thanks to all in H1920 who long ago taught me what was needed.

In "A Search for Glenn Gould", the voices in Tracking appear, as it were, in this order: Janet Somerville, William Aide, Norman Snider, Michael Pepa, Ken Freed of *The Los Angeles Times*, of course Glenn Gould himself, and Mrs. G.K. Brady.

Reference to Wyndham Lewis's Canadian passport is found in the introduction to *Wyndham Lewis: An Anthology of His Prose* (1969) by E.W.F. Tomlin. I am indebted to Hugh Kenner's *The Pound Era* (1971) for biographical information about Lewis; to Fredric Jameson; to George Steiner's essays on post-literacy, especially *In Bluebeard's Castle* (1971); to Walker Percy's *Lost in the Cosmos* (1983), an unjustly neglected work; and also to Susan Sontag's fine essay "Mind as Passion", which helped to introduce me to the work of Elias Canetti; last, Collins Publishers in Toronto for the Canetti books themselves, and for many Canetti quotations, which are scattered throughout the text.

TSO was written between April 1984 and December 1986. All exaggerations, omissions, and errors are mine; no one else can be or should be blamed.

B.W.P. Toronto, December 1986